'The world of life, of spontaneity, the world of dawn and sunset and starlight, the world of soil and sunshine, of meadow and woodland... of wildlife dwelling around us, of the river and its wellbeing – all of this [is] the integral community in which we live.'

Thomas Berry

Creative team

Contributors

Images

Editor-in-chief
Carole Bamford

Creative Director
Claudie Dubost

Editorial Director
Imogen Fortes

Editorial Assistant
Lisa Perry

Digital Content Editor
Catriona Collins

Production Coordinator
Matthew Gorman

Words
Leonora Bamford
Catriona Collins
Will Dennis
Phoebe Hunt
Sir Nicholas Kenyon
Fiona McCarthy
Tatsuro Miki
Harriet O'Brien
Ben Olsen
Lizzie Rivera
Jez Taylor
Anna Turns
Axel Vervoordt

Recipes
Adam Caisley
Gaven Fuller
Dominique Park

Photography
Clay Banks
Valentino Funghi
Laziz Hamani
Arindam Mahanta
Lizzie Mayson
Miti
Jocelyn Morales
Martin Morrell
Paulo Sousa
Wycliffe Stutchbury
Edwin Tan
Eric Tourneret
Lisa Tse
Simon Webb
Julian Winslow

Styling
Milly Bruce
Claudie Dubost
Frankie Unsworth

Illustration
Marc Majewski
Iris de Moüy

Printed in the
United Kingdom.
Colour management
and print production
by Completeltd.com

© Carole Bamford 2022
All rights reserved.
Reproduction of the
whole or any part of this
publication is prohibited
without express written
permission of the publisher.

Cover photography by
Martin Morrell
@seed_magazine

Contents

10
in conversation with Justin Byam Shaw
The founder of The Felix Project discusses the driving force behind his food redistribution charity, which works to redress the balance between Londoners struggling to afford to eat and the city's surplus of edible food

14
natural highs
With communities of wild swimmers springing up around the world, we look at the benefits to be gained from taking the plunge – from a sense of shared experience to invigorated mental health

18
our daily bread
Bread making has enjoyed a resurgence, with home bakers rediscovering the simple pleasures of a fresh loaf. As many expand their repertoire, we consider why opting for heritage grains has benefits for the soil – and ourselves

26
when the music stops
The pandemic forced many musicians to lay down their instruments and severed relationships with audiences. As live performances resume, we consider the role music has to play in a time of crisis and what the future holds for the next generation of young artists

34
into the blue
Where better to look for wellbeing advice than the five places on earth whose populations live the longest? We explore the common features of the world's healthiest communities

38
tracing the grain
Crafted using fallen timber, Wycliffe Stutchbury's intricate and immersive works reveal a considered, sensitive appreciation for his material

48
restoring the balance
It's as important as the oxygen we breathe, but do we really know what our lymph is or how to look after it? We share simple ways to nourish and support the fluid that bathes and replenishes our bodies

50
the rise of urban beekeeping
From the roofs of London galleries to the tops of New York skyscrapers, beehives are cropping up in the unlikeliest of places. We talk to one of the urban beekeeping movement's earliest pioneers

56
eat well
A selection of seasonal recipes reflecting our belief that to eat well is to eat locally, in season, organically and without waste

72
how sustainable are our coffee choices?
Whether you take yours black, white, filtered or frothed, there's no avoiding the fact that coffee consumption has a consequence. We investigate the widespread impact of our caffeine habit and how we can choose a more responsible, sustainable cup

76
wabi
Art collector Axel Vervoordt's restrained interiors reflect his admiration for the Japanese culture of wabi. In this extract from his book *Wabi Inspirations*, Vervoordt explains the philosophy that celebrates the beauty in imperfection

84
pastures new
One of England's largest protected areas is enjoying a reawakening. From conservation projects to panoramic supper clubs, we share the ventures that are breathing new life into the rolling Cotswold countryside

92
on the up
A sustainable and efficient growing solution, or a nutritionally devoid food system that ignores the needs of our soil? We consider the reasons to support or to shun the wave of vertical farming projects

96
growing tomatoes successfully
Learn how to grow your own summer tomatoes with a guide from Jez Taylor, head of Daylesford farm's market garden

100
growing a garden meadow
Not only will wildflower seed bombs help keep the bees happy, they're a brilliant way to keep little hands busy. Make your own following our easy step-by-step guide

104
a table for spring
A collection of wildflowers, crockery and colour to inspire a seasonal table setting

Seed likes

A BOOK

Every Family Has a Story
by Julia Samuel

|

A PLACE

Warleigh Weir
Claverton, England

|

A PODCAST

River Cafe Table 4
Ruth Rogers

|

A TABLE

Hjem
Hexham, Northumberland, England

|

AN EXHIBITION

Our Time on Earth
Barbican Centre, London

Editor's letter

As we began planning our fourth volume of *Seed*, there was a sense that the world was turning a corner. We could begin to recalibrate our lives, to reconnect and reimagine a future beyond the restrictions and rules.

Often we look back to decide what to take forward, and in reflecting on our shared experience of the past few years, what struck me is that the pandemic urged us to unite. The sense of collective purpose in battling a common affliction gave us connection, strength and faith. We clung to that feeling of togetherness and came to understand its value.

With that in mind this issue of *Seed* considers the sense of belonging and feeling of security that come from being part of a community. Our writers reflect on the communities that have been born out of this period of crisis, bonding over shared interests or intentions. We discover what lies behind the longevity and happy lifestyles of the world's healthiest communities, and we also consider the effects on the communities that were torn apart: the musicians and performers who were forced to regroup to find new means of reaching their audience and fill the void left by this sudden severance.

Communities thrive because interconnection underpins our existence as humans. As we continue to seek the solutions that will determine a more sustainable future for our earth, I hope that this issue inspires you to remember how connected we are to each other and to nature. Our actions impact those around us and they impact our planet, our shared home. Progress is achieved when we share knowledge and experience, and act and work together as one.

– Carole Bamford

daylesford
× COLEFAX

@DAYLESFORDFARM   WWW.DAYLESFORD.COM

IN CONVERSATION WITH
JUSTIN BYAM SHAW

WORDS Carole Bamford
PHOTOGRAPHY Lisa Tse

Justin Byam Shaw is the founder of The Felix Project, the London-based food redistribution charity set up in memory of his son Felix who died suddenly from meningitis in 2014. It rescues nutritious, good-quality surplus food that cannot be sold and would otherwise go to waste. Around 1.5 million adults in London struggle to afford to eat every day and 400,000 children are at risk of missing their next meal; meanwhile, the food industry generates millions of tonnes of good, edible surplus food each year. The Felix Project works to solve both issues. In 2020, the organisation provided enough food for 21 million meals. It had never seen such high demand for food as during the Covid-19 pandemic and had to vastly expand its operation to meet the need for its services.

The numbers indicating the enormity of The Felix Project's response during the Covid-19 pandemic are phenomenal – what was the scale of the increase?

Just before Covid began we were providing food that amounts to the equivalent of 6 million meals a year [The Felix Project assumes a meal to be 400g of food]. In 2021 we achieved over 30 million meals. We expanded by nearly fives times over Covid and we're continuing to grow. Another development was the launch of our own kitchen. Some of the surplus food we collect is diverted to our kitchen and made into nutritirious meals, typically for children on free school meals in East London.

You had to react to increased demand almost immediately; what was it that enabled you to extend the support and the help you offered at such immense speed?

There were two factors. Firstly, I was chairman of the Evening Standard at the time, and I went to speak to the owner, Evgeny Lebedev, in March 2020 and said that things were looking really bad in London. In the first month of lockdown a million people in the UK applied for Universal Credit, so it was pretty clear to me what was going to happen – there were going to be huge hunger problems. Evgeny agreed that I should speak to the paper's editor, George Osborne, who decided to run

'All this wasted food is a massive environmental fail. Around 8 per cent of the greenhouse gases in the world are generated by food that was grown and then wasted.'

a year-long campaign called 'Feed London Now'. The campaign's aim was to raise £1 million but by the end of March we'd raised £3 million and George felt we should keep going. By the end of the year we'd raised £10 million, which was astonishing. That is the principal reason why we were able to fund a hugely ambitious plan to increase from 6 million to 30 million meals. Individuals, companies, chefs doing special events, Damien Hirst, Peter Blake and other celebrities giving us items of real value to auction, people running the London marathon, restaurants putting money on the bill – all these fundraising efforts, which all happened very quickly, raised a huge amount of money.

The second catalyst was the extraordinary financial support we had received over the prior three years from the Quintessentially Foundation and the supportive celebrities they brought into our orbit. This had given us the confidence to start the planning for growth, so we were well prepared.

How many volunteers do you have normally?

We now have about 1,500 but some will only come in occasionally, some of them twice a week. We're a voluntarist organisation – it wouldn't work without people giving us their food and people giving us their time.

How easy is it to attract volunteers?

We do get a constant stream of new volunteers but we always need more. It's easy for potential volunteers to understand what we do and why and that makes us attractive. People like to work in the warehouses or help cook in the kitchen, but the volunteers we probably need most are people who will drive our vans to collect and deliver food.

It's an extraordinary kind of volunteering because after two hours you've felt like Father Christmas: you've picked up a load of amazing food from Daylesford in Pimlico, say, and you have taken it to a local homeless shelter and a drug rehabilitation centre; you can see the benefit of what you're doing instantly and that's quite unusual.

Did you feel that the communities you were reaching or needing to reach during the pandemic changed?

Yes, definitely. I remember making a delivery to an organisation that runs a soup kitchen in Trafalgar Square called Rhythms of Life. I went along in April 2020 and was staggered by how the queue was about 10 times the size of what it was normally – it was snaking down and round the streets around Trafalgar Square. That was a very visible demonstration to me of the enormity of the problem the pandemic had caused. Normally there about 20 people in the queue; there seemed to be about 200, and not all of these looked like the people you might expect to be in a queue for soup. It was very striking and pretty moving.

Loneliness was another huge problem during the pandemic – do you think you saw an uplift in demand for food and people coming to soup kitchens

because sharing meals helped bring people together?

Yes, I do. I always say that our food is food for the soul as well as for the body. We are part of the social kitchen, Refettorio Felix, at St Cuthbert's in Hammersmith, and it's obvious to me that the people that go there do so because they're lonely. You see people who are smartly dressed, and you realise they could afford to buy the food but they are there because they're lonely or have a mental illness which has isolated them. You definitely notice the value of providing a meal in company as opposed to sending it to someone's home. We even gained some volunteers during the pandemic because of people wanting social interaction at a time when there wasn't much.

What do you feel are the biggest challenges facing charities such as The Felix Project, but also charities more widely?

For charities in general – not so much mine – there have been statutory funding cuts by government and a number of small charities are really struggling to survive. Why do I know that? Because many charities we supply have an income of below £100,000, and if your income is less than that and you get a government funding cut then you're on the breadline yourself; you're really struggling and I know that there are quite a few organisations we deliver to who wouldn't survive without our food. There's a knock-on effect in the community. There have been a number of small charity closures throughout Covid and I'm sure there will be more over the next year, as demand grows and funding dries up further. Also Covid has diverted money in particular directions and not others.

For us the main issues are recruiting ever more volunteers to support our ultimate goal of a London where no one goes hungry and no food is wasted and accessing good-quality food. There's a crazy situation in this country where only 7% of the vast amount of edible surplus that's generated by the food industry gets to charities; the other 93% goes into landfill, gets burned in an incinerator or goes to an anaerobic digestion plant to become fertiliser. There's more than enough food to go around; it just doesn't reach the right people.

At the moment it's often easier for a food company to send its surplus to landfill and anaerobic digestion plants. In France they have a law preventing that. Big food companies are obliged by law to offer their edible surplus to charities first, before they can dispose of it in any other way. And the result of that is that 10 times as much food reaches people who need it in France than in the UK. I'm not sure similar legislation would work here but we do think large food companies should be obliged to publish their food waste stats, so that their consumers, shareholders and the media can see how they are doing. I am sure this would result in a significant reduction in waste, with more of it given to charity.

The government gives huge subsidies (£600 million p.a.) to the anaerobic digestion industry. And an unintended consequence of that is that all this great edible surplus food, which could be eaten, becomes crop fertiliser. The other point is that it's not just a social and economic concern; all this wasted food is a massive environmental fail. Around 8 per cent of the greenhouse gases in the world are generated by food that was grown and then wasted. Think of all the water and energy that is required to grow that food and then you burn it or you put it in landfill; it's such a scandal that hasn't really surfaced yet, but it will.

A third of the food produced in the world is wasted. That's equivalent to landmass the size of China being given over to food production and then that food being wasted. Our grandchildren will look back on the way we've behaved and ask how we could have done this? How could we have let that happen to the environment?

NATURAL HIGHS

WORDS Phoebe Hunt
PHOTOGRAPHY Clay Banks

The adrenaline rush, the potential health benefits, or simply as a life-affirming tonic for mind and body: these are just some of the reasons that devotees cite to explain the appeal of swimming in open water. Over the past few years the draw has become ever more enticing; increasing numbers of us are taking the plunge. With communities of cold-water swimmers springing up around the world, Phoebe Hunt discovers the irrevocable joy and sense of a shared experience that lie behind the call to swim in the wild.

I came to love sea swimming during childhood summers in the Isles of Scilly, a scattering of remote islands and craggy rocks off the Cornish coast, which have some of the coldest seas in the UK. Unprotected by the mainland and ruled by strange currents and tides, the azure waters can turn perilous in an instant; the white sand beaches and shallows at once idyllic and sinister. Countless sailors have lost their lives around these picturesque shores over the centuries, flotsam and cargo salvaged by islanders when it washed up on the beaches.

It is with respect and no small amount of fear, therefore, that this deep love of the open water has stayed with me into adult life. Through break-ups and life decisions, I, like so many others, am drawn to bodies of water wherever I can find them: secluded lakes and waterfalls, icy winter beaches and public lidos. The appeal of outdoor swimming – the allure of taking that icy plunge – is deeply primitive. It's the adrenaline rush; the electricity that surges through your body; the all-round physical wellbeing, and the dramatic immersion in nature that we often lack in everyday life. As award-winning travel writer and environmentalist Daniel Start wrote: 'All wild-dippers know the natural endorphin high that raises mood, elates the senses and creates an addictive urge to dive back in. However the world seems before a swim, it looks fantastic afterwards.'

Over the last decade in particular, there has been a huge resurgence in wild swimming – the flashy term for what humans have always done. This comes in no small part from writers such as Roger Deakin, whose elation is infectious as he describes the 'frog's eye view' of the UK, swimming his way through the country's rivers, lakes and canals in a mad quest for happiness. In 1996 and in his early fifties, Deakin started writing his seminal book, *Waterlog*, which has inspired a generation of swimmers. 'I wanted to follow the rain on its meanderings about our land to re-join the sea,' he wrote, 'to break out of the frustration of a lifetime doing lengths.'

'I can dive in with a long face and what feels like a terminal case of depression and come out a whistling idiot.' Roger Deakin, *Waterlog*

There is something gorgeously irreverent about some of the places where Deakin chooses to bathe. Indeed, his most poignant descriptions are not of idyllic brooks, but are more often when he mourns the loss of the natural world, after a swim in a contaminated stretch of water. One bittersweet chapter describes a sludgy swim in the River Lark in Suffolk, which old-timers remember as 'sparkling and transparent', home to otters and water voles. Deakin finds the river poisoned, polluted, and boxed into a concrete channel flowing through a parking lot.

Artist Emily Ponsonby references Deakin a lot as inspiration for her paintings, using layer upon layer of oil and beeswax to capture the beauty of warm bodies plunging beneath the silky waters of a pond, river or wave. 'It's not about speed or elegance but about a longing to wriggle free of clothes and sink into an icy undiscovered watery realm. Weightless, bare-skinned and tingling we re-enter a womb-like state where survival, rather than life's silt, becomes the dominant aim. Water snakes, newts and frogs look on with curiosity, rather than fear, at the large smooth creatures coinhabiting their watery home. For me, this is why I love swimming outside; for we are reminded of our place on earth.'

Scientifically, there are many suspected health benefits to swimming in cold water. Research into the so-called 'cold shock' protein RBM3, detected in the blood of a group of regular winter swimmers at Parliament Hill Lido in London, has shown tentative links with slowing dementia. Multiple claims have also been made about the benefits of regular cold water immersion boosting the immune system, increasing the white blood cell count, reducing stress and increasing libido. Though most of these claims are anecdotal, the number of people who have transformed their lives by cold water swimming is certainly compelling.

Wim Hof, nicknamed 'The Ice Man' for his superhuman ability to withstand freezing waters with only the power of his mind and self-styled breathing techniques, is one of the more outlandish of these devotees. His exploits include a near-fatal 57-metre swim under ice, and immersing himself in a tub of ice for almost two hours. Arthritis, Crohn's disease and chronic inflammation are among the conditions he claims can be helped by the stimulation of cold water immersion.

Closely connected to this are the countless stories of people suffering from chronic depression and anxiety finding solace and even a cure in wild swimming, and imploring others to do the same. Deakin is one such advocate, returning time and time again in his writing to the way a sort of mental metamorphosis happens when you leave the land behind. The British Medical Journal has published details of a small handful of cases in which open water swimming has successfully treated people suffering major depressive disorders, on occasion allowing individuals to come off conventional medication completely.

While these success stories should be read with caution, what is indisputable is that wild swimming has seen an unprecedented surge in recent years. In 2006 the Outdoor Swimming Society had 300 members; they now have over 100,000 across the globe. According to Sport England, a national organisation that promotes physical exercise, some half a million people in England were regularly taking dips in outdoor spots by 2020. A whole community has built up around it, something Ponsonby describes as, 'a shared feeling of absurdity that forms a tight bond between a pod of swimmers'. In the UK, groups such as Chilly Dippers gather in Edinburgh for gleeful winter swims followed by bacon butties, while in Manly, Australia, Bold and Beautiful Swim Squad meet every morning to swim together.

Beyond claims of wellness, it's the sheer joy of taking outdoor plunges that is behind its enduring popularity. Reading the accounts of authors like Deakin and Margaret Drabble, co-author of *At the Pond*, it's tempting to rush to the nearest lake and strip off, but swimming in open water is perilous even for experienced swimmers and should not be taken lightly. With caution, it can be a tonic for body and mind, a physical immersion in nature that forces us to stop and be totally present as we splash around with glee. In short, there is no greater feeling of being alive.

ARTISTS, POETS AND WRITERS WHO CELEBRATE WILD SWIMMING

ROGER DEAKIN
Author of *Waterlog – A Swimmer's Journey through Britain*

EMILY PONSONBY
Cotswold-based painter who uses oil and beeswax to create swimming scenes

MARY OLIVER
20th-century American poet, whose works include *Waterfall* and *The Swimmer*

DANIEL START
Author of *Wild Swimming: 300 Hidden Dips in the Rivers, Lakes and Waterfalls of Britain*

MARGARET DRABBLE
A lifetime devotee of swimming at the Hampstead Ladies' Pond, and co-author of *At The Pond*

OUR DAILY BREAD

WORDS Catriona Collins - PHOTOGRAPHY Martin Morrell

A more efficient way to farm land and a nutritious way to feed a nation, the virtues of growing and baking with heritage grains are as far-reaching as the root systems on which they thrive – and finally the home baker is catching on. As our appetite for artisanal ingredients and 'real bread' grows, we visit Gilchesters Organics's mill in Northumberland to find out what makes their flour so beneficial for our bodies and our soil – and how bakers' enthusiasm for different types of flour could see the emergence of a local grain network near you.

Calming yet stimulating, meditative yet satisfying, bread making is a ritual as old as time. It took on new levels of importance during the first few months of the Covid-19 pandemic, providing comfort and security during a period riddled with uncertainties. When many of our simple pleasures had been stripped away, baking was a pastime that enabled us to keep busy, produce, and experience excitement – no matter what was going on outside the walls of our kitchens. From nurturing sourdough starters, kneading glutenous dough and tucking bread babies into banneton baskets, to patiently monitoring their growth, savouring the yeasty aroma and hungrily devouring that first, butter-laden slice, there is fulfilment to be found at every stage. Channelling our energies into the rhythm of these tasks gave many a sense of positive control; a reassuring and stabilising force even when the ground underneath us felt shakier than ever.

This feeling of cosiness extended far beyond our 250°C ovens and piping-hot loaves, with a global community of bakers emerging online. On 30th March 2020, just days after the UK went into lockdown, mere mentions of bread on Twitter doubled in number from over 80,000 to over 180,000 per day, while 'sourdough' and 'banana bread' became the most searched-for recipes on Google during 2020.

Alongside a newfound connection to fellow bakers, lockdown was a time when we engaged more deeply and meaningfully with the natural world around us. Our pace slowed, our eyes opened, and daily walks and window-gazing encouraged us to appreciate the easily overlooked beauty of nature. Shortages on supermarket shelves not only prompted us to shop more locally, but also raised questions around the UK's food system, and the sustainability of where our food actually comes from, including how crops are grown. At its core, bread making is nothing more than the alchemy of three simple ingredients: water, salt and flour – the last offering the most opportunity for experimentation, nutritional value and flavour variation. As with any mass-produced store-cupboard staple, not all flours are equal, something the wheat geneticist and organic miller Andrew Wilkinson firmly believes. 'There is no nutritional value whatsoever in roller-milled white flour,' he says. 'None. There is more nutritional value in your corduroy shirt.' It is with this conviction that he and his wife Sybille turned their conventional cereal farm in Stamfordham, Northumberland over to an organic system in 2000.

Following two years of regenerating the soil, enrolment in an organic wheat research PhD programme at Newcastle University, some sage advice on heritage cereal varieties from Swiss plant breeders, the installation of a volcanic Naxos milling stone and the acquisition of a local miller, Gilchesters Organics was born, and in 2005 they began milling the heritage grains grown in their rich organic soil just meters away.

Today the farm grows a variety of single-estate heritage grains and cereals, meaning the crops have a lineage and purity that can be traced back to before WWII, after which a need for quantity over quality led to intensive plant breeding and genetic modification. By contrast, Gilchesters' older 'heritage' grains are a strain of the original hardy crops grown on this land, with Andrew and Sybille seeking to reintroduce the 'vitality, vigour and architecture of these wonderful plants back into today's farming arena,' not least because their resilience makes them better suited than modern varieties to cope with weather fluctuations driven by climate change. Gilchesters' current varieties include heritage wheat grains, as well as rye, spelt and even older emmer and einkorn cereals. Their most recent addition is buckwheat, a response to the growing demand for gluten-free options.

Nutritional density is at the heart of why the couple believe so deeply in the virtue of the grains they grow. Having looked at plant breeders across Norway, Austria and Switzerland, Andrew found early research work identified a link between straw height, nutritional density and baking quality when grains were grown under organic conditions. A need to 'feed the world' post-war forced farmers to prioritise the size of a crop's harvest over its nutritive value, leading to the use of chemical growth regulators, such as chlormequat, that bring the plant height down, thus diverting the crop's energy

'The deep rooting systems of heritage wheat varieties are also beneficial for the soil.'

away from its straw and root system, and maximising it in the grain-bearing ear of the plant instead. Though this increases the yield, Andrew describes these crops as nutritionally void – reliant on the chemicals they were fed rather than the soil that was nourishing them. The effect is exacerbated during the processing system, with a national desire for white flour pushing millers to strip away the grains' nutrient-rich bran casing and wheat germ and discard an alarming 30 per cent of the crop to produce the familiar, highly refined white powder we all depend on so heavily. In turn, this supports a style of agriculture that is neither efficient nor sustainable.

The long-strawed, heritage varieties of grain Andrew has been experimenting with for the last two decades are infinitely more nourishing, containing more protein and fibre, and micronutrients, such as vitamins and minerals. 'With each step we take to reintroduce these heritage cereals back into our diets, we are producing a more efficient and nutritionally-dense food system, meaning we can actually have a greater impact on our health and digestion while eating less.' There is a reason we can easily inhale multiple slices of buttered white toast, and yet if you eat a proper wholegrain slice, one is usually enough. The grains give the bread a low glycaemic index, more chewing is required and the density in nutrition and texture mean that hunger is properly sated. As Andrew points out, 'There is the capacity to feed the world using the earth's landmass – if we adjust what it is we are growing.'

Rye is the gold-standard grain in terms of nutritional density; it contains a significantly higher level of antioxidants than any other heritage cereal. Couple this with the slew of benefits that come from eating the fibre-rich bran and vitamin-rich germ of a whole grain and it is 'one of the best grains you can put in your body', comments Sybille. It is also why she insisted on travelling to the UK from her home in Bavaria with a bag or two of the precious milled grain in her suitcase before rye became readily available in the UK.

Beyond how they can improve the health of humans, farming these grains organically also has a host of wider ecological benefits. Andrew finds that sightings – or sounds – of owls are the best indicators of biodiversity, and is happy for them to wake him at various hours of the night if it means his farm's ecosystem is in good working order, flourishing with mice, beetles, slugs and their various predators. An estimated 14 kilometres of unworked 'habitat corridors' that connect Gilchesters' fields mean that there is also an array of lapwings, curlews, buntings and other birds making themselves at home among the natural nesting sites.

Not only taller than modern-bred wheats, the remarkably deep rooting systems of heritage varieties are also beneficial for the soil, enabling the plants to scavenge much further into the earth. This ability to access a deeper reservoir of nutrients combined with rotational farming ensures that Andrew's soil 'recycles nutrients in a way that enables us to top up what we've taken out, rather than deplete them irreparably from the soil.'

As with all organic farming, Gilchesters' mission to preserve these heritage varieties comes with its hardships, and the often-hostile Northumbrian weather is their main, unavoidable aggressor. Andrew describes 2019 as a 'horrible year' in terms of farming activity, the soggy end of which left him unable to sow rye, einkorn and emmer, forcing him to preserve these seed stocks for kinder growing conditions rather than risk potentially losing the lot. Despite this, there is contentment to be found in 'enjoying the fact that it's not all perfect', says Andrew, who philosophically affirms that 'we are so intrinsically bound to the natural world around us', a reality so often overlooked in conventional farming. Ancient grains can also be low-yielding, and tall grains, such as spelt, whose hard-to-reach kernels remain in their casing are, in Andrew's words, 'a pig of a thing to harvest'. Developments in modern farming machinery are encouraging, however, and technology such as 'spelt settings' on combine harvesters now makes things significantly easier than when Gilchesters first started.

It seems as though our newfound nation of bread makers is possibly as ecologically and nutritionally mindful as Andrew and Sybille. Gilchesters saw remarkable growth during the lockdown baking revolution – during March 2020 they experienced a 700 per cent increase in orders. Although this hysteria has calmed down somewhat, the home baker has now overtaken restaurants as their biggest financial support, with over 300 new customers continuing to order regularly and a surge in demand for their whole, unmilled grains indicative of domestic experimentation with miniature countertop mills.

Andrew believes we now have a 'taste and feel for proper bread', and it is a trend that looks set to stay. As we begin to look beyond the supermarket shelves, provincial artisan bakeries are also clamouring for homegrown flour, leading to a resurgence in local grain networks all over the UK. There are also smaller-scale millers, farmers, crop scientists, breeders and bakers working together to share knowledge, and offer an appetising alternative to large-scale agricultural production. This organic and natural groundswell of interest is incredibly encouraging, indicative of consumers' desire to feel connected to where their food comes from; and – a sentiment at the heart of everything Gilchesters seek to achieve – to retain the value of the landscape within the community itself.

'With each step we take to reintroduce heritage cereals back into our diets, we are producing a more nutritionally-dense food system.'

WHEN THE MUSIC

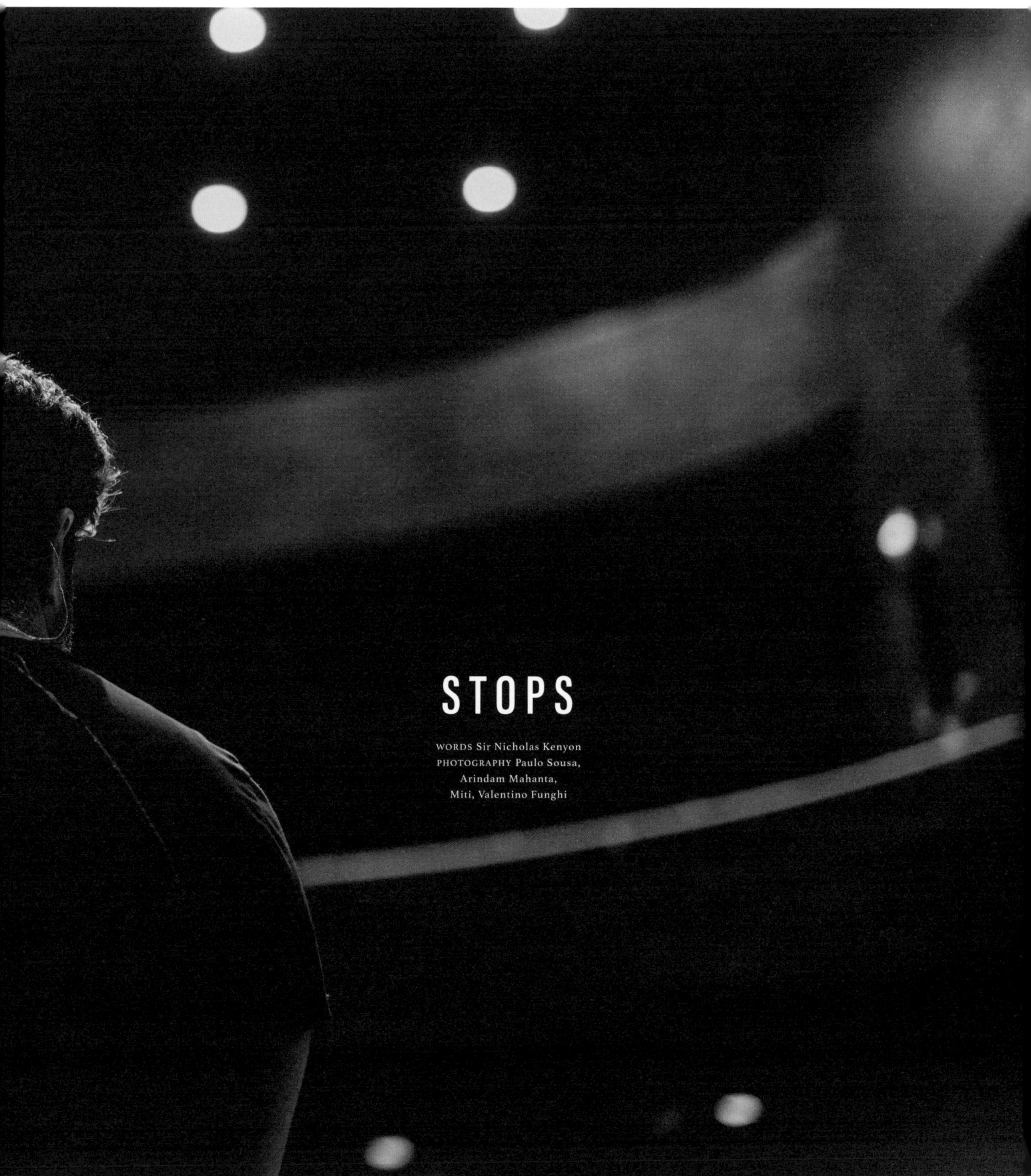

STOPS

WORDS Sir Nicholas Kenyon
PHOTOGRAPHY Paulo Sousa,
Arindam Mahanta,
Miti, Valentino Funghi

Sharing music is about communication and community. Musicians perform to and convene with an audience and when that bond is severed, their very essence and purpose is taken away. Over the past 18 months musicians have been forced to innovate and regenerate to find new and creative ways of connecting with their listeners. As live performances resume and ensembles come back together, we consider how musicians have weathered the global pandemic and what the future holds for the next generation of artists entering the profession.

Music brings us together. So many of the great occasions in our lives, from weddings and memorials to coronations, funerals and festivals, are bound together by music as a profoundly unifying force. We may not count ourselves as musical, we may not have the skills to participate – though often that does not stop us from joining in – but we are inextricably linked together and moved by the power of music.

For 12 years I had the privilege of running the BBC Proms at the Royal Albert Hall, and night after night crowds would gather to share the experience of great music in a unique arena. There was always a special atmosphere in that circular space, where audience and performers could see each other clearly and be aware of each other's presence: it swept them together into one community. There were powerful moments when, as a national event, the Proms had to respond to the public mood. In 1997, the death of Diana, Princess of Wales brought mourning crowds to Kensington Gardens just outside the hall. We had to adjust both the mood and the programming over the days that followed – though as it happened we had already programmed Verdi's *Requiem*, said to be Diana's favourite piece of classical music, for the penultimate night of the season, it served as a memorial both to her and to Sir Georg Solti who had died earlier that week. We adjusted the high spirits of the Last Night, and had to do the same in 2001, when the attacks of 9/11 in New York occurred just days before the end of the season. By leaving out some of the more nationalistic elements, adding Barber's sombre *Adagio for Strings*, and the finale of Beethoven's utopian 'Choral' Symphony, we transformed the concert into a powerful tribute.

In times of crisis, music has something essential to offer. At the height of the blitz during the WWII, Dame Myra Hess famously mounted concerts in London's National Gallery and drew audiences, even though the paintings themselves had been moved to safety in the Welsh mines. Music reflected our resilience and determination. Arguably there has been no greater challenge to our national life since that war than the wholly devastating pandemic of 2020/2021. Yet during this crucial period, the situation was different. Music could not respond. The pandemic turned on its head so much that we had believed about the unifying power of music. Suddenly our survival depended on *not* coming together, on *not* gathering, and on isolating safely away from other people. We were all victims in that process, but those who suffered with particular force were those who made music their living. The pandemic tore apart a pattern of rehearsal and performance, private practice and public appearances, teaching and travel, recording and concerts – a demanding yet a sustainable way of life.

Some musicians were fortunate enough to remain employed, but many who worked freelance suffered a devastating loss of income. Some retreated into silence, other fought to preserve their identity and practised furiously. Some relished the chance to spend more time with their families, others played in small ensembles outside so they could be socially distanced. It was fascinating to see the many different creative reactions to the situation. Artists are by nature inventive and ingenious, so new initiatives blossomed. Freelance musicians' support groups sprang up online. Individuals multitracked themselves on recordings (my favourite early video was of Peter Whelan singing two vocal parts, playing the bassoon and the keyboard, to create an exquisite Bach cantata duet). Choirs could not rehearse together, but they could record their individual parts separately, creating the amazing 40 parts of Tallis's famous motet *Spem in Alium* in digital form in a beautifully edited version that showed the different voices entering and leaving.

For big venues forced to close, the effect of the restrictions suddenly imposed around the pandemic was devastating. The Royal Opera House in London's Covent Garden had to cancel a performance of Verdi's *La Traviata* on the day lockdown began with only a couple of hours' notice. They then had to abandon plans to show Beethoven's *Fidelio* live in cinemas and cancelled the dress rehearsal of a new production of Janáček's *Jenůfa* (though the staging was reassembled in late 2021). The Royal Opera House had to revert to the streaming of opera and ballet from their catalogue to keep in touch with their audience, a worthwhile offer but not one that could replace the thrill of newly created work.

Some organisations refused to be defeated by the pandemic. As one example among many, an especially adventurous initiative came from Leipzig, where in 2020 the annual Bach Festival had aimed to bring together choirs from all over the world. Instead, they made specially prepared small

'In times of crisis, music has something essential to offer. The pandemic turned on its head so much that we had believed about the unifying power of music.'

arrangements of two great Bach works, the *St John Passion* and the *B Minor Mass*. They performed the *St John Passion* around Bach's grave at St Thomas's Leipzig on Good Friday, and then the *B Minor Mass* during the period of the festival in June. These were given with minimal live performers in Leipzig, but they invited Bach choirs from around the world to join them online in some of the choruses and chorales. The results, now edited together and issued on a DVD called *#BachBeatsCorona*, are deeply moving.

London's Barbican Centre used the period when audiences were not allowed in the building to create new digital work that had socially distanced musicians performing in some of the different spaces in the famous modernist building, using the foyers that are usually crowded with audiences. Experimentation allowed the creation of more sophisticated ways of televising performances, with special lighting and staging allowing cameras to move around the hall and building a stage out into the audience area for the wonderful pianist Benjamin Grosvenor. Gradually, small socially distanced audiences were allowed back in, and artists of the stature of Bryn Terfel, Sarah Connolly and Ian Bostridge were able to return to performing live within the restrictions.

But for those whose engagements had disappeared completely during lockdown, work only slowly began to recover, and by then it was too late for some. When one orchestra decided to put together a concert to support freelance musicians when activity began

to resume, they were shocked to find that colleagues were not available because they had abandoned the profession. They were working in supermarkets and surgeries, driving delivery vans etc. When, during the 2021 Proms, the BBC assembled a Proms Festival Orchestra consisting entirely of freelancers who had come back to playing, the stories they told of jobs they had been doing ranged from working in a vineyard to working in a funeral parlour, taking up woodworking, and founding a local small-scale music festival.

Mark Wigglesworth, who conducted that orchestra in a rapidly-assembled performance of Mahler's *Fifth Symphony*, had a very honest line: 'There's a loneliness as much as there's a privilege to being a freelance musician.' The question is now what the long-term damage could be from this whole period. A year ago, there was disturbing evidence from the Musicians' Union that up to a third of professional musicians across the genres were considering changing jobs and would be forced to find new jobs when support schemes ended. Now the situation is more positive because opening up is proceeding, ensembles have reunited, and audiences are flocking back to communal experiences.

As halls and operas houses have reopened, and musical events around the UK have resumed, it has been encouraging to see how enthusiastically they have been received by packed audiences. Performances have had an extra added dimension of thrilling excitement for the artists, as they returned to the work they longed for. Every orchestra and ensemble has experienced that sense of relief and renewed sense of purpose. It remains to be seen whether the insights and practices that have been developed during the pandemic in the area of digital transmission, creating new ways of harnessing technology supported by on-line subscriptions, will help to create a new economic model for music-making. These routes enable the online work of musicians and ensembles to find ever-widening audiences at home and abroad, especially for those without easy access to local venues.

I have recently talked to students at the music colleges who are about to emerge into the profession: at the start of the pandemic they were full of uncertainty about whether their chosen route into music-making was going to be destroyed. Now they are optimistic that new opportunities will open up for them, and that the older established members of the profession who have laid down their instruments during the pandemic may decide not to pick them up again, creating vacancies in our established orchestras. But they recognise that there are other major challenges to musicians' lives which have become inextricably linked with the pandemic, and are radically affecting the work that they will be able to do: the impact of Brexit, the lack of music and the arts in schools, and the urgent need to increase the diversity of the profession. It is impossible to disentangle these concerns from the impact of the pandemic; they all point towards more radical change in the musical profession in the coming years.

Change (to echo the words of the famous hymn '*Abide with Me*') is not always decay. Rather it can provide the spur to new thinking, and that is surely what the pandemic has provided. The cultural world needs to recognise that the world as a whole is changing radically around it, and the most imaginative musicians will embrace this in the way they organise their lives and grasp the opportunities of this new world. The inspiring music director of the Philadelphia Orchestra, Yannick Nézét-Seguin, said as they re-opened Carnegie Hall in New York in October 2021: 'We must perform on our stages everything the world has to offer.'

That is a rallying cry which says that the endless riches of music are there to be discovered: old music will be reinterpreted by a new generation of performers, new music will be created by our young composers, and the full diversity of the classical tradition must be reflected in our programmes going forward, encouraging a new generation of young people to engage creatively with the art form. The results may not be a return to the old normality of musical life, but they will offer audiences a reinvigorated and renewed musical life.

Sir Nicholas Kenyon was Director of the BBC Proms 1996–2007 and Managing Director of the Barbican Centre 2007–2021. He is the author of The Life of Music: New Adventures in the Western Classical Tradition *(Yale University Press).*

INTO THE BLUE

WORDS Ben Olsen
ILLUSTRATIONS Marc Majewski

Coming to terms with our mortality is part and parcel of growing up but longevity is something we can all strive for. This is where groundbreaking research identifying the world's Blue Zones® – the five regions whose populations live the longest – has a part to play. We consider the wellness lessons to be learned from the world's healthiest communities.

> 'If you live in a community that has strong bonds and lots of social interaction, you get a "longevity dividend".'

Perhaps now more than ever before, we're starting to recognise the importance of taking care of our wellbeing. The pandemic has put into sharp focus just how much our lifestyles affect our overall health while, thankfully, more and more companies are making efforts to prioritise the wellbeing of their employees. As we collectively begin to consider the factors that contribute to healthier, happier lives, lessons can almost certainly be drawn from the communities that comprise the world's Blue Zones®.

First appearing in a National Geographic feature by journalist Dan Buettner in 2005, the term is used to describe the regions of the world where a significant number of people live much longer than average. Buettner's work, which built upon the findings of scientists Gianni Pes and Michel Poulain, centres on five Blue Zones®, whose name nods to the blue concentric circles Pes and Poulain originally used to highlight these areas on maps: Okinawa in Japan, Barbagia in central Sardinia, Costa Rica's Nicoya peninsula, the Greek island of Icaria and Loma Linda, California. In all five geographically distinct locations, the population's life expectancy is higher than usual, but what unites them?

One scientist familiar with the concept of Blue Zones® is longevity expert Professor Ian Philp, adviser to the World Health Organization and the UK government's former tsar for older people. 'This research captured the global attention as a concept that popularised the lifestyles in certain parts of the world and it's a great way to demonstrate this to people in a visual way,' he says of Buettner's work, which identified nine specific lifestyle habits (see opposite) that these five areas share. 'Lots of academic teams have since gone into the Blue Zones® and tried to work out the factors that contribute to the longevity phenomenon in each of them.'

Philp has analysed Buettner's list of nine behavioural and environmental factors alongside subsequent research and views the most important factor for a longer life as being a sense of social connection. 'If you live in a community that has strong bonds and lots of social interaction you get a "longevity dividend",' he says, noting how many western societies have become more atomised, with these connections made weaker as a result. Just about equal in importance, he adds, is breathing clean air, with toxic fumes shortening life expectancy, while he also emphasises the positive effect of integrating exercise into your daily routine. 'In central Sardinia, which has the longest life expectancy for men in the world, the terrain is very hilly. Most of the men being studied there are shepherds and the fact that they're traversing this hilly terrain all their lives is a key factor in their longevity,' he says. 'While not all the Blue Zones® are hilly, they all involve people being active in their daily lives.'

The verdant Nicoya Peninsula in Costa Rica's north-west boasts of having the highest number of centenarians in the world. According to Jorge Vindas, founder of the Nicoya Blue Zone Association, physical activity plays a major role in this. 'Many of our elderly grew up in an environment where the jobs of men and women were very physical, using the machete and the axe, working on horseback, walking long distances to go to work,' he says. 'And while there are now more home comforts, many of our oldest survivors still move about in their daily activities.'

Vindas observes that these hardy communities also tend to grow their own food using organic principles. 'From cultivated fields to the pot, possibly the most important thing here is the consumption of food with little or almost no processing, he says, outlining a diet based on rice, beans, pork, chicken, plenty of corn and vegetables such as cassava, tiquisque (yam) and sweet potato. Yet the importance of diet to our longevity can be rather nuanced, as Philp explains. 'While the Mediterranean diet – lots of vegetables, fruit, nuts, pulses, fish – is fantastic, in some of the Blue Zones®, people also eat lots of fatty meat,' he says. 'For me it's how you eat that matters. In most of these areas, this is often communally – they sit down and take their time, have good conversation and eat slowly. They eat to enhance life rather than eating to cope with stress.'

Managing stress is often measured in how well you sleep and a common theme in the Blue Zones® is that people often have full and active days with a good night's sleep at the end of it, which is particularly restorative for the body. Mental agility plays its part, too. According to Philp, engaging your brain can create neural circuits that slow the onset of dementia while delivering greater alertness and a more active mind, which help you to cope with life better. As with Buettner's original research, Philp sees having a sense of purpose as another uniting factor – if we know who we are and why we're on this planet, we continue to do things that give life meaning. Finally he notes the importance of self-esteem. 'People who think they look old become depressed and less active. Looking after your appearance and developing positive self-esteem is important,' he says. 'You see that in the Blue Zones® where there is joy at being alive at 90.'

This last point resonates particularly in Japan, where Professor Masashi Arakawa from the University of Ryukyus explains the Okinawan tradition of Kajimaya – an event celebrating those who reach the age of 97, who are said to be reborn and return to being a child. 'The whole town celebrates this birthday and the star of the day will hold windmills and parade in convertible cars through the village,' says Arakawa. He has helped develop the new Blue Zone Stay at the Hoshinoya Okinawa hotel, which offers guests the chance to experience some of the wellness principles in perhaps the most famous of Buettner's Blue Zones®. 'Longevity is a source of pride for long-lived people here, who are recognised for their experience, knowledge and wisdom, and are seen as a treasure to the community.'

It's a powerful sentiment and a reminder of how differently those in other parts of the world treat their elderly. Is this why a developed country such as the UK tends to have lower life expectancy by comparison? 'There are lots of reasons why we don't do as well – we often lose the joy of connection, we have more sedentary lifestyles, we're exposed to more pollution, we eat and drink to cope with stress rather than to enhance pleasure, we lead busy stressful lives and don't sleep as much,' says Philp. While adding that our advanced healthcare systems mean we are living longer now in the UK, Philp is confident that we could gain an extra five to 10 years if we adopted Blue Zone® lifestyle principles.

His advice is to consider the Blue Zone® principles in the context of your own life and decide which you're able to change, with simple adaptations – whether learning new skills, making changes to your diet, taking up a sport – potentially delivering benefits. 'Some things are tricky – if you live in a polluted place and are unable to move away, at least try to take breaks in the year where you can go away and rest your heart and lungs,' he says. 'For me, I was ignoring my wife's advice to use moisturiser for years. I made that simple change and feel better about myself as a result – I look younger!'

There are limitations and caveats with the Blue Zone® research – these locations are evolving swiftly with the arrival of western diets and modern trappings making life easier, which in turn is affecting longevity. There's also the importance of genetics with many scientists finding that the genetic makeup of people in particular Blue Zones® provides inherited longevity benefits that can't be learned. However overall, the concept provides compelling grounds to prioritise our wellbeing. 'Our centenarians have shown that their lifestyle works. We must learn from them and adapt as much as we can to the modernity that can drown us so rapidly,' says Vindas. 'It is our responsibility to teach younger generations about these extraordinary people while understanding how important it is to lead a calm life – I feel the closest word to happiness is tranquility.'

BELONG

LOVED ONES FIRST

80% RULE

WINE @ 5

PLANT SLANT

RIGHT TRIBE

MOVE NATURALLY

PURPOSE

DOWN SHIFT

TRACING THE GRAIN

WORDS Fiona McCarthy
PHOTOGRAPHY Wycliffe Stutchbury, Simon Webb

A passion for the idiosyncrasies of natural timber – weathered, fallen or forgotten – drives the intricate, immersive works of British artist–maker Wycliffe Stutchbury. We meet him in his London studio to discuss the boundaries and conceptual thinking guiding his work.

Standing tall and lean, dressed in a tawny workman's coat blemished a little by the wear and tear of carpentry dust and wood glue, Wycliffe Stutchbury's gentle demeanour lends a softening touch to the otherwise basic surrounds of his workshop. Located off a cobbled mews, the small studio is surrounded by a community of painters, ceramicists and glassblowers, at the back of an old suitcase factory in south London.

Here, walls are neatly hung with the tools of his woodworking craft, from saws and chisels to clamps; shelves heave with pieces of timber, both found and sculpted; and a large bandsaw and long worktable dominate the space's centre. It is 'the perfect retreat', he says, for an artist – or rather, maker, as Stutchbury prefers to be described – working in solitude.

'The way I understand it, art is about an idea for which you then find the most appropriate materials to execute, while craft is more about technique and respecting the material,' he says of where he sees himself falling within the art versus craft debate.

After a career making furniture for more than two decades, in the last 12 years Stutchbury has become one of the leading lights in the British craft world, where his fastidiously detailed, immersively captivating works are now highly sought-after (and priced accordingly) around the world.

Hundred Foot Drain 7
(triptych, left panel) 2019

Stutchbury's vast tiled works, made up of thousands of hand-cut tiles – 'painstaking in their thinness,' he says – in the shapes of matchsticks, rectangles and squares (some no bigger than a fingernail), are hypnotic in the way they intimate a sense of landscape, providing what feels like a bird's eye view of alluvial plains, meandering rivers, fields and valleys. 'The initial quality you are struck by in these pieces is colour, then line, then form or relief, and finally texture,' he enthuses. 'My work has become more like painting, but with tiles.'

Conversely, his sculpted pieces, fashioned from solid pieces of fallen or felled common holly, horse chestnut or ancient bog oak, some bleached a little and sanded smooth like plaster, feel almost anatomical in nature, visceral in their resemblance of femur bones and spinal cords. 'The first time I cut into holly I had no idea that it was so pure because it's such a tough tree,' says Stutchbury of the wood he has used for recent pieces such as Brass Point 2 and The Hill 9. 'The bark looks like elephant's skin, the leaves are prickly, everything is saying don't come near; but then you cut into it to discover it has the most beautiful close grain, like ivory, and the colours are fantastic,' he says.

Stutchbury first started working with wood as a teenager, despite the fact that he and his art teacher 'didn't get on', he laughs, 'but I loved doing things with my hands.' When he first left school, he pursued being a musician, playing the clarinet and saxophone, until 'I realised I wasn't as committed as the other students who were sleeping with their violins.' Instead, he applied his long, slender fingers so perfect for scaling the keys of a sax to the fine art of furniture-making. Following a course at the London College of Furniture in the late eighties, an apprenticeship with Rod and Alison Wales, of Lewes-based Wales & Wales, taught Stutchbury 'everything', he says. 'There it was about line, and timber, and while beautifully executed it wasn't unnecessarily detailed.'

Having then done the rounds of furniture-making, exhibition building and kitchen fitting for many years, 'I knew I didn't want to end up being stuck in a manufacturing workshop, becoming a slave to overheads, taking any job to survive,' he says. 'I always had the idea that I was going to do something low tech, to deconstruct and make things simpler – the bandsaw is the only key piece of equipment I have – and the quality of the making experience has been so much improved by just being able to sit at the bench with the quiet.'

Stutchbury resolved to make pieces 'that hung on the walls because people have space on their walls, and I'd seen how friends in the industry had struggled to sell functional pieces of furniture,' he recalls. His first piece was conceived

Royal Hospital Chelsea, 2020

Brass Point 2, 2020

'Everything is saying don't come near; but then you cut into [holly] to discover it has the most beautiful close grain, like ivory.'

entirely by chance. 'Walking home one day, past a house being re-roofed, there were all these timber batons weathered in amazing colours of rich browns and reds lying in the front garden,' he remembers.

He took them, chopped them up and experimented with the pieces like a collage. 'My first work was called West Terrace – after where I'd found the wood – and it was a completely regular, straight arrangement of the tiles, highlighting the colours, which I framed in glazed mahogany,' he says. He liked its museum exhibit feel and 'that was the start of it all.' A couple of years later, exhibiting at the Crafts Council's then Origin: London Craft Fair in 2009, his first collection of wall hangings sold out immediately. He was awarded Best Contribution to Show and garnered enough further orders to keep him going for a year.

Further shows with the Murphy Machin Gallery at the Affordable Art Fair, the Woolff Gallery on Charlotte Street and the Flow Gallery in Notting Hill established his reputation as a serious contender in the crafts world. More recently, showing with Sarah Myerscough Gallery, his work has been elevated to global acclaim, recognised by leading institutions such as The Wood Awards, Jerwood Makers Open and the Loewe Craft Prize.

Having gone back to university to complete a BA (Hons) in 3D Crafts from Brighton University in 2003, today Stutchbury's craft draws on all those earlier learned furniture-making techniques but is combined with the artistic sensibility of knowing 'when to stop and allow the timber to speak for itself,' he says. For each piece, he is led by the characteristics of the timber in front of him – 'it's just wonderful to respond to the character of a material,' Stutchbury continues, 'and although I love its unpredictability, it is also unreliable and full of surprises. It splits, it cracks, it warps, but I've tried to celebrate that.' For instance, in some of the pieces like the spheres (Peelings Barn 2), 'I've imposed this geometric form on a lump of wood but then allowed it to do its thing,' he says, highlighting the way the deep fissures within the wooden ball threaten to tear it apart.

There is a two-fold ethos underlying this talented maker's works. 'It is not just about the finished timber, but also about paying homage to these amazing trees and how they have adapted to their environment and the scars they've sustained,' he says. 'Just think of those majestic plane trees in an old London square that are simply towering over us and observing, watching us running around; they're vastly wiser than we are,' Stutchbury reflects. Or the hawthorn trees on the South Downs, being tortured and swept away by the prevailing wind. 'They just dig in their heels and grow at extraordinary angles. They record time.'

His practice is defined by a set of self-imposed boundaries. Each piece is made from a singular source of timber – one work might be made from stripping away the weathered top layer of a batch of fence posts, another from a single

Far left: The Rodd 3, 2019
Felled European Oak
Powys, Wales.
20cm

Left: Peelings Barn 1, 2019
Fallen Horse Chestnut
Hankham, East Sussex
16cm

fallen or felled tree – and then named after where it was found, tying the work to a sense of provenance and place. For his tiled works, he embraces the limited palette the batch of timber presents. 'If there was infinite choice, I wouldn't know what to do,' he confides.

The 'little idiosyncrasies' of colour – caused by being underground for hundreds of years or perhaps weathered in places where a gate latch might have been – make the crafting process more appealing. 'I've become increasingly interested in what the eye is drawn to, so I keep some imperfections in there,' he explains. 'If they're subtle, they add to the piece in a natural way; if they are too big, they become distracting.'

Working with fallen timber allows him to play with a further narrative: 'opening it up and revealing the story inside the wood,' he says. 'There'll be wounds, there'll be discolouration and rot.' For instance, in last year's solo 'Fall Line' show at the Sarah Myerscough Gallery, Stutchbury showed a standing piece sculpted from fallen holly, looking very much like a knee bone, where he embraced 'the incredible strength and tension you could see in the way the wood had broken'.

Predetermining scale is another limitation he sets for his tiled works, purposely challenging his practice further when he might suddenly find himself dealing with a tight corner where he won't allow himself to simply snip away any overhanging wood strips. 'I like the starting point it gives me, because being told what size to make a piece might restrict its format but not the freedom of how I work within that,' he muses. When he feels he's getting too intensely wound up in the making of a piece, 'I also enforce false deadlines on myself just because that last hour before you have to go home is the freest, or I work with really low light levels so I can only just see, or I even take my glasses off so I really can't see, to loosen me up,' he laughs.

While Stutchbury crafts his pieces to incite curiosity and adventure, 'I don't want people's first reaction to be "wow, how did he do that?",' he says. 'I like the idea of a piece being mesmerising and someone always being able to find new places to go within it – I like the way you get this initial overall experience and you're taking it all in, but then you start to close in on particular areas and see the individual components and then start following those,' he furthers.

'I've been doing this for over a decade now, and I haven't by any means reached the end of the road of laying one tile after the other,' he says. 'Even doing panels, I have loads of ideas of what I want to do there.' From a series of triptych screens, standing almost two metres tall, which Stutchbury showed a few years ago at Collect (the leading international art fair for contemporary craft and design) to new textile pieces which resemble something akin to a curtain of cowhide, where he has pitted the rigidity of tiny wooden tiles against the fluidity of cotton twill, there seems to be no bounds to Stutchbury's work.

Gayles Farm 5, 2020
Photograph: Simon Webb

RESTORING THE BALANCE

WORDS Fiona McCarthy · ILLUSTRATION Iris de Moüy

It's an invisible system that gives us vitality and replenishes our bodies to ensure we are the healthiest versions of ourselves, yet how many of us know what it is or how to look after the fluid at its heart? We investigate the benefits to be gained from supporting and keeping our lymphatic system in balance and how we can best take care of it ourselves.

When it comes to fuelling mind, body and soul, there is always much (valuable) talk about the importance of getting enough sleep, nourishing our bodies with antioxidant-rich foods, maintaining good gut bacteria, stretching our limbs and building our bones. Yet there is often little mention of how to look after our lymph, the magical fluid that constantly replenishes our bodies, and which is as important as the oxygen we breathe and the blood that pumps through our veins.

According to Lisa Levitt Gainsley , author of *The Book of Lymph: Self-Care Lymphastic Massage to Enhance Immunity, Health and Beauty* (Yellow Kite) published in September 2021, each of us has 'an invisible system that is continually working beneath the surface, connected to every inch of our body, tidying up and sending vitality and support to ensure we are the most radiant and healthiest version of ourselves.' This is our lymphatic system and flowing constantly through it is lymph.

In simplest terms, lymph works to drain the fluid that surrounds all the cells in our bodies' tissues; protects our bodies from disease by removing germs (bacteria, viruses and parasites) and toxins (poisons); helps to destroy cells that are old, damaged or abnormal; and absorbs fats and vitamins from our digestive systems, transporting them back into our bloodstreams. 'Every cell in our bodies is literally bathed by its fluid. It's the often-overlooked missing link to vibrant health,' Levitt Gainsley enthuses.

Think of it like a network of tiny streams flowing into rivers – lymph isn't pumped around the body by the heart but pushed along when the lymphatic vessels are squeezed by our muscles (and by gravity, if the vessels are above the heart) – which then drain into lymphatic ducts, before emptying into the bloodstream, toxin free, via large veins near the heart.

More scientifically, according to Lymphoma Action (lymphoma-action.org.uk), the hundreds of lymph nodes in areas such as our necks, armpits, knees, groins, chests and stomachs help to filter lymph. They trap germs and damaged or abnormal cells by activating immune responses to help the body get rid of them via white blood cells called lymphocytes, which multiply inside the lymph nodes, fighting the infection and making chemicals that activate other parts of our immune systems.

Or, in Levitt Gainsley's words, the lymphatic system 'acts like a garbage collector, sweeping immune cells through your body to weed out anything that threatens your wellbeing, making lymph your first line of defence against illness.' When it functions properly, 'you feel vibrant, energetic and clearheaded,' says Levitt Gainsley, a qualified lymphedema therapist, who started her own private practice in Los Angeles in 2001. 'When your lymphatic system is congested, you might feel lethargic or stuck, constipated and headachey, experience more aches and pains than usual, and find you're more susceptible to colds.'

There are multiple benefits from looking after our lymphatic system, especially given it is connected to every other system in the body including the nervous, digestive and neurological systems. A healthy lymphatic system improves the body's fluid balance, reduces blood pressure and inflammation, and can even keep weight on track. Hollywood star Tracee Ellis Ross (Diana Ross's daughter and star of *Black-ish*) swears by dry body brushing for when she's feeling tired or sluggish, the perfect way to fire up both blood and lymph circulation as the bristles help to remove dead skin cells, boosting a healthy blood flow and stimulating lymphatic fluid drainage. Model and businesswoman Elle Macpherson heads straight to her lymphatic drainage masseur to help combat jetlagged abdominal puffiness; and the actor Selma Blair, diagnosed with multiple sclerosis in 2018, heads to Levitt Gainsley when she wants to 'reconnect her tired body with the hum of life.'

Understanding our lymphatic system isn't new. Hippocrates, the Greek physician was one of the first to mention the lymphatic system in his fifth-century BC work *On Joints*, but it wasn't considered seriously until the seventeenth century, when Swedish scientist Olaus Rudbeck was one of the first to pioneer the study of lymphatic vessels, supported further by the work of the eighteenth-century Scottish anatomist Alexander Monro who first described the function of the lymphatic system in detail.

In the 1930s, a manual technique for lymphatic drainage massage – a non-invasive system of gentle, rhythmic and pumping movements, concentrating on the fluid found just under the skin and much gentler

HOW TO SUPPORT YOUR LYMPHATIC SYSTEM

than deep-tissue body work, designed to reduce swelling in the lymph nodes – was developed by Danish doctor Emil Vodder and his wife Estrid, a naturopath, while working in France. More recently, studies on the human brain revealed it has a lymphatic system of its own and by understanding the way the body's lymphatic system works to eliminate waste and infection, it brings hope that doctors might use this knowledge to also understand how to encourage the brain's lymphatic clearing system, helping to improve the lives of those suffering with conditions such as Alzheimer's disease.

There are several easy things you can do to encourage better lymph (the Latin word 'lympha' referring to the deity of fresh water 'Lympha'). For Levitt Gainsley, her advocacy of lymphatic self-massage is 'a little like feng shui-ing your body,' she suggests, referring to the ancient Chinese philosophy of harmonising the flow of energy around one's physical surroundings. Her book outlines multiple lymphatic drainage massage techniques you can do at home to address different health concerns. 'Getting your gut flowing by massaging your abdomen improves digestion and helps you to feel much clearer; massaging the head and neck helps to lift brain fog and headaches; massaging your diaphragm keeps your lungs functioning properly,' Levitt Gainsley enthuses. Along with breath work and exercise, it's clear that she considers looking after our lymphatic health is as important as eating and sleeping well, that we need to do it on a daily basis to be 'the most radiant and healthiest version of ourselves.'

DEEP DIAPHRAGMATIC BREATHING

The movement from breathing alone provides an invaluable means for oxygenating the blood and circulating lymph. Place both hands on the stomach. Breathe in through the nose for the count of five, then breathe out through the mouth for five; rest between breaths and repeat five times. Even if you do this for just 10 minutes a day (try it in the morning, after you've woken up but before you've jumped out of bed) it will make you feel fantastic.

HYDRATE

General advice is to drink 6–8 glasses (or 2 litres) of purified or filtered water a day; start the day with a mug of warm water laced with lemon; avoid sugary soft drinks, stick to herbal teas and black coffee.

DRY BODY BRUSHING

Try the classic ayurvedic ritual known as 'garshana', which helps to remove dead skin cells and improve skin circulation, just before you shower, by working a natural bristle brush towards the heart in light, long strokes, starting from the feet upwards for the lower body, and from the hands for the upper body, paying particular attention to where you have lymph nodes (neck, armpits, knees, groin, chest, and stomach). Go gently around the neck and décolletage, brushing downwards towards the heart, and finish by going over your heart in a circular motion. Or repeat the same motions with a soaped-up soft loofah in the shower.

MOVE

Lymphatic flow relies on movement to action the contraction of skeletal muscles which forces the tiny one-way valves of the lymph system to open and close, helping lymph to flow around the body. Even just a 30-minute walk at lunchtime will help, as will doing a series of arm raises and knee bends every day, some yoga or Pilates stretches, or going for a swim.

EAT WELL

Minimise processed foods and unhealthy fats and up your intake of: rainbow fruits and vegetables (especially chlorophyll-rich greens); nuts (such as almonds and walnuts); fresh herbs and lean protein (such as poultry, fish, beans and pulses).

NATURAL BEAUTY

Minimise parabens, sulphates, silicones, petrochemicals, synthetic fragrances and preservatives in your skin and body care products, as well as in daily household cleaners, and where possible, choose natural organic fibres (cotton, wool, cashmere, linen) for clothing, bedding and soft furnishings.

MEDITATE

Reducing the acidic waste products released by stress-fighting hormones will help to avoid lymph congestion. For helpful guides to meditation and mindfulness, try apps like *Calm* and *Headspace*; or enrol in one of Bamford's wellness retreats in London or the Cotswolds.

THE RISE OF URBAN BEEKEEPING

WORDS Will Dennis
PHOTOGRAPHY Julian Winslow (this page), Eric Tourneret (overleaf)

City rooftops may not seem like the most obvious draw for flower-loving pollinators, but in recent years beehives have become an increasingly common sight on urban skylines. Despite the challenges of keeping bees up high, businesses and hobbyists have been embracing the artisanal craft and celebrating the complex flavours of honey produced from a diversity of nectar. We meet one of the earliest pioneers of the urban beekeeping movement to learn why it's still going strong and whether its intention to support biodiversity and climate action efforts is proving effective.

Bees are remarkable creatures, honeybees in particular. Even for the uninitiated, few people fail to marvel at the mathematically flawless hexagonal comb that bees create; fewer still can resist the allure of a jar of amber honey. With a work ethic almost unparalleled in the natural world, each bee works tirelessly to ensure the future of the hive. Foragers fly as far as five miles from home in search of the best nectar, and on their return will communicate its exact location to their fellow workers through a unique routine known as 'the waggle dance'. A healthy, productive hive will quickly expand and produce honey, and it is for this liquid gold that we have been keeping bees since the last Ice Age. More important, however, is bees' role in global food production. Three quarters of the crops we grow depend on pollination. Put simply, bees are an essential part of human survival.

It is alarming then that bee populations are in rapid decline across the world. This is in part due to widespread use of pesticides, which pose a severe threat to all pollinators and the vital ecosystem service they provide. One group of insecticides in particular – neonicotinoids – has been linked to bee decline. These chemicals have been in use since the 1980s, and were once relied upon for maintaining the vast, beautiful yellow fields of oilseed rape in our countryside. Unlike most spray-on pesticides, they are applied as seed coatings and affect every part of the plant, including nectar and pollen. 'Neonics' are chemically similar to nicotine and cause paralysis and death in pests by targeting the nervous system. However, they were also found to be affecting non-target species such as bees, leading to their ban in the EU in 2013.

In the early 2000s, there was a surge in beehives appearing in the unlikeliest of places – on our city rooftops. Many of these were hobbyists using a private terrace to house a small hive, but there was also the arrival of curious commercial beekeepers keen to experiment with urban nectar. One man responsible for leading this movement in the UK was Steve Benbow, owner and founder of the London Honey Company. 'I had always toyed with keeping bees in London,' recalls Steve, who was a beekeeper in his home county of Shropshire for many years before the effects of the insecticides in

nearby rapeseed fields forced him to look elsewhere. 'Huge piles of our bees were appearing in front of the hives on sites close to oilseed rape,' he says, as dying or paralysed bees took themselves out, or were evicted from the hive. 'I just knew there was something wrong. I wanted to return to London, away from intensive agriculture.'

Steve started with a single colony on the roof of his flat in Bermondsey in 1999 with the aim of 'bringing a little bit of countryside to the capital'. 'Back then, no one was keeping bees quite so centrally and I was surprised by how well they did but also how incredible the honey was.' He quickly noticed that, quite unlike the increasingly monofloral countryside at the time, urban environments offered a diverse variety of nectar which created a wonderfully complex honey. Initially concerned that he 'would be producing something that would be toxic', Steve was amazed by its floral taste and tests showed it to be free of pollutants. His business was born as the demand for local food grew.

The rise of beekeeping also saw the resurgence of a cottage industry with the demand for its equipment. 'In the

UK it's still lots of people working out of their sheds and building things themselves,' says Steve, who saw 'a healthy craft industry being rejuvenated' by beekeepers supporting small local businesses. As well as woodworkers to create frames for the hives, artisan candlemakers emerged to trade in the new sources of beeswax. There is even a market for bespoke designer hives, which Steve uses for some of his specialist rooftop projects. 'There are some really amazing craftsmen out there,' he says.

Despite the appetite for their honey, bees themselves have not always been popular. Steve's own bees were evicted by the council, who banned him from keeping them on his roof. In a previous career as a photojournalist, Steve had encountered beekeepers in cities around the world including Rio and Paris. He remembers experiencing similar resistance on his visits to the guerrilla hives of New York City, where 'honeybees had to be kept very covertly,' as they were considered illegal wild animals by the authorities. Urban beekeeping became a clandestine operation for a group of hardy individuals, until changes in public perception led to bees becoming more widely accepted.

'Bees are now considered to be the glamorous pin-up of the pollinator world,' says Steve, whose business expanded with the increased requests from companies to have bees installed on their rooftops, many of which Steve still services. Although business has grown Steve chose not to expand the number of rooftop hives too heavily and limited the service offered, recognising that this was not a business that should have huge expansion. Today the London Honey Company has hives scattered across the UK, in quite unique locations that they actively seek out.

Steve is proud to be the bee master for Fortnum & Mason, responsible for managing their four sophisticated Piccadilly hives, along with a portfolio of exclusive sites that includes the Royal Albert Hall, the Tate galleries and the Royal Estates. In return for supporting the pollinators with safe roof space they receive their own 'hyper-local' honey to sell in their gift shops.

©Cultura Creative RF / Alamy stock photo

Beekeeping is a true artisan craft, requiring exceptional levels of patience and dedication. As the urban craze for keeping bees took off, many of its new adopters hung up their smocks after their first season, put off by the commitment it demanded and lack of immediate reward. 'It was a bit of a trend and then people realised it's actually really difficult keeping bees in an urban environment,' says Steve. Commercial honey operations struggled to find new recruits, and this confirmed fears that beekeepers were an aging population. As Steve recalls, 'there was a real wake-up call for the industry that a lot of great knowledge was being lost with these incredible mature beekeepers.' An apprenticeship scheme was launched in response in 2014 and strong partnerships with schools were established. Bees now feature in several topics of the UK National Curriculum, including symmetry in nature, learning about pollinators and food production.

Although the initial flurry of interest appeared to have died down, it left a strong legacy. 'What remains is a lot of great beekeepers and associations with communities in cities,' says Steve, 'and these bodies are really good at getting people involved and making sure they adhere to good practices.' Early years education and mentoring are proving successful, and along with hiring apprentices Steve himself has passed on the art of beekeeping. 'It's very much a family business now,' he says; his nephew has also joined the London Honey Company.

The future is uncertain for bees. An increasingly unpredictable climate causes variable honey yields with warmer, drier weather threatening the availability of nectar. 'A real concern is that the weather patterns are changing and becoming more uncertain,' says Steve, who admits that the higher temperatures in cities will be especially challenging. Competition for resources is an added threat, with recent studies finding that some urban areas have inherited too many bees. 'We are very conscious not to overpopulate an area and we want to avoid overwhelming other pollinators,' says Steve, though his intentions may not be shared by amateurs unaware of the potential damage they can cause.

Hope lies, however, in the burgeoning movement of nature-friendly activity and awareness in cities. 'There's a fantastic change in the way that people are thinking about their own window boxes, backyards and community spaces,' says Steve, who has also seen stark changes in the countryside. Indeed, in the decade since he published *The Urban Beekeeper* (an engaging anecdotal guide for new keepers), production of the monocrops that prompted his move to London has dwindled. Landowners have embraced rewilding and cover cropping methods, allowing rural pollinators to thrive once again. In our cities the authorities have become advocates for bees, and hives are encouraged in allotments and parks where once they were outlawed. New York City now boasts huge rooftop vegetable and salad gardens providing new forage opportunities for their legalised bees. Even Steve's London council had a change of heart: 'they actually came back to me a few years later and said they'd like me to put my bees back.'

The recent lockdowns have seen a revival of interest in beekeeping, and Steve's company were quick to move their courses online. 'We were finding that whole families wanted to learn about it, and we sent out honey tasting kits for them to try,' he says. As restrictions lifted more people attended the courses in person, where the team instils the importance of responsible practice. Like other well-intentioned movements in support of biodiversity or climate action, beekeeping can still be a viable hobby provided that the right guidance is followed. Buying local food should always be encouraged if it has been produced with a conscience.

Reflecting on a life of bees, Steve credits them for his success. 'They have given me so much,' he says, 'from mental wellbeing to a successful business; I would have nothing without my bees.'

> 'There's a fantastic change in the way that people are thinking about their own window boxes, backyards and community spaces.'

www.thelondonhoneycompany.co.uk

Late spring and early summer bring waves of edible arrivals to the garden. There are the vibrant greens – pea shoots, spring leaves and the first asparagus – then as summer settles in, the warmer days bring forth a riot of colour as radishes, rhubarb, strawberries and heritage tomatoes begin to dominate our plates.

There is an ease to cooking at this time of year. Mealtimes are occasions for assembly rather than watching pots. These recipes celebrate that simplicity. Sharp, bright dressings, a drizzle of olive oil or the gentle backdrop of a creamy risotto or comforting tart filling illuminate and support, allowing the garden's heroes to shine.

RECIPES Gaven Fuller, Adam Caisley and Dominique Park
PHOTOGRAPHY Lizzie Mayson
FOOD AND PROP STYLING Frankie Unsworth

Rocket gnocchi

with roasted tomato and balsamic sauce

SERVES 4

1.1kg King Edward potatoes (should give you about 550g cooked flesh)
handful of rock salt
150g plain flour, plus extra to dust
90g semolina
50g rocket, finely chopped
5 medium egg yolks, beaten
30g butter
sea salt and black pepper
freshly grated Parmesan, to serve

FOR THE ROASTED TOMATO AND BALSAMIC SAUCE

2 white onions, finely chopped
3 tbsp olive oil, plus extra to serve
2 garlic cloves, finely chopped
2 tsp finely chopped thyme leaves
950g cherry tomatoes, halved
1 tbsp balsamic vinegar
3 tbsp chopped parsley
2 tbsp chopped mint

METHOD

Preheat the oven to 180°C fan.

Wash and thoroughly dry the potatoes and pierce each with a knife. Sprinkle a little rock salt over the centre of a baking tray and place the potatoes on top. Bake in the oven for about an hour until cooked through.

Meanwhile, make the sauce. Place the onions in a medium saucepan with the olive oil. Cook over a low heat to sweat and soften them without letting them colour. Add the garlic and cook for a few more minutes, then add the thyme. Add the cherry tomatoes and continue to cook slowly for 5–10 minutes until the tomatoes have started to soften. Add a splash of water, some salt and pepper and continue to cook for a further 5 minutes to allow them to break down.

Remove from the heat, add the balsamic vinegar, then the parsley and mint and finally add a drizzle of olive oil and stir. Set aside.

When the potatoes are ready, sift the flour into a large bowl and stir through the semolina, rocket and some salt and pepper. While the potatoes are still hot, cut them in half and scoop the flesh out of the skin. Pass the flesh through a ricer or coarse sieve into the bowl.

Add the egg yolks to the bowl and stir everything until it just comes together to form a thick dough. Do not stir the mixture too much as this will make your gnocchi chewy.

Dust a clean work surface with flour and turn the dough out from the bowl. Roll into a sausage shape around 2cm in diameter and cut with a sharp knife into 3–4cm long strips to form your gnocchi. Place on a baking tray dusted with flour.

Bring a large pan of water to the boil with a generous pinch of salt. Turn down to a simmer before gently dropping in about a quarter of the gnocchi. Stir carefully with a spoon and wait as they gently rise to the surface. As soon as they come to the surface, remove with a slotted spoon and place in a bowl. Repeat with the remaining gnocchi.

Heat the butter in a large shallow frying pan until bubbling. Add the gnocchi and fry until they begin to turn golden brown. Add enough of the tomato sauce to coat lightly and toss everything together. Divide between four plates and serve with a generous scattering of Parmesan.

The rocket can be substituted for basil or spinach leaves. The sauce will make more than you need but it freezes well so making a big batch is a great way of preserving any bountiful crops of tomatoes.

Tomato and broad bean salad
with anchovy dressing

SERVES 4

50ml olive oil
25ml vegetable oil
20ml sherry vinegar
10g Dijon mustard
½ garlic clove, crushed
¼ shallot, finely chopped
25g tinned salted anchovies, finely chopped
200g broad beans, podded
500g mixed tomatoes (ideally heritage varieties of varying shapes and sizes)
sea salt and black pepper

METHOD

To make the dressing, whisk the oils, vinegar, and mustard in a small bowl until well combined. Add the garlic, shallot and anchovy and set aside to infuse while you prepare the salad.

Place the broad beans in a saucepan of boiling salted water. Return to the boil and simmer for 2–3 minutes, until the beans are just tender. Drain and cool under cold water. Once cold, slip off the tough outer skins.

Cut the tomatoes into wedges and arrange in a serving dish, seasoning lightly with salt and pepper. Add the broad beans, then drizzle over around half of the dressing quantity, or more to taste.

The dressing quantity is double the amount you will need but it can be kept in the fridge for up to 3 days.

Broad bean and cannellini dip with peas and mint
served with roasted beetroot

SERVES 4

250g podded broad beans (or use frozen)
250g frozen petit pois
2 tbsp tahini
1 x 400g can cannellini beans, drained and rinsed
2 garlic cloves, crushed
juice of 1½ lemons
100g feta
50g mint, finely chopped
sea salt and freshly ground black pepper
olive oil, to serve
small handful of micro herbs, to serve (optional)

FOR THE ROASTED BEETROOT

400g beetroot, washed
drizzle of olive oil
splash of balsamic vinegar
large pinch of thyme leaves

METHOD

Preheat the oven to 180°C fan. Place the beetroot on to a large square of foil. Add a drizzle of olive oil, the thyme, balsamic vinegar and some salt and pepper. Wrap the foil tightly around the beetroot.

Place the foil parcel on a roasting tray. Roast for about 40 minutes, until just tender and cooked. Remove the beetroot from the foil and once cool enough to handle, gently rub away the skins, then cut into wedges and transfer to a serving dish.

While the beetroot is in the oven, place the broad beans in a saucepan of boiling water. Return to the boil and simmer for 2–3 minutes, until the beans are just tender. Drain and cool under cold water. Once cold, slip off the tough outer skins. Blanch the peas in the same way.

Place the broad beans in a food processor along with the peas, tahini, cannellini beans, garlic and lemon juice and whizz until smooth. Add the feta and mint, season and whizz to combine.

Transfer the dip to a serving bowl, drizzle over a thin layer of oil, then cover and chill until ready to serve. The dip can be kept in the fridge for up to 3 days. Scatter with micro herbs, if using, and serve alongside the warm roasted beetroot.

Broad bean, pea and asparagus risotto

SERVES 4

80g butter
1 tbsp olive oil,
 plus extra to serve
350g carnaroli rice
75g onion,
 finely chopped
1 garlic clove
120ml dry white wine
600ml hot vegetable
 stock
220g broad beans,
 podded
200g peas (frozen
 or fresh)
200g asparagus
80g grated Parmesan,
 plus 15g shavings
 to serve
large pinch of sea salt
20g pea shoots
sea salt and black
 pepper

METHOD

Melt 40g of the butter with the olive oil in a large heavy-bottomed saucepan. Add the onion and garlic and let them sweat gently without colouring on a low–medium heat. Add the rice and let it sweat for 5 minutes, stirring all the time.

Pour in the wine, increase the heat and leave the wine to bubble until all the liquid has evaporated then add the hot stock a ladle at a time, continuing to stir. Repeat until all the stock has been absorbed then season to taste. The rice should still have a little bite to it. Lower the heat to the lowest setting.

Meanwhile, place the broad beans in a saucepan of boiling water. Return to the boil and simmer for 2–3 minutes, until the beans are just tender, adding the peas for the final minute. Drain and cool under cold water. Once cold, slip off the beans' tough outer skins.

Add the broad beans, peas and asparagus to the pan of rice, then add the Parmesan and remaining butter, stirring vigorously to work the risotto and warm the vegetables. Leave to rest for 30 seconds, then serve in bowls. The risotto should still be wet enough to settle into the shape of the bowl with a wave-like motion. Top with the shaved Parmesan and the pea shoots and then drizzle with olive oil. Finish with black pepper.

Vegetable scraps, such as peel and trimmings, are often just considered waste and end up in the bin, but we can reframe that thinking. Trimmings can be saved and used to make vegetable stock. The best way to do this is to store them in a sealed bag in your freezer until you have a hefty enough quantity to go into a stockpot. Be sure to wash them before freezing – and look out for mud or dirt in onion skins, and the tops and roots of other vegetables.

Crab tart
with summer leaves

SERVES 6-8

300ml double cream
200g brown crab meat
3 eggs, plus 1 egg yolk
Tabasco, to season
Worcestershire sauce,
  to season
pinch of cayenne pepper
sea salt and black pepper
pea shoots, to garnish
mixed summer leaves,
  to serve

FOR THE PASTRY

250g plain flour
125g unsalted butter
pinch of salt
1 medium egg, beaten,
  plus another, beaten
  for the egg wash

FOR THE TOPPING

175g picked white crab meat
2 spring onions, finely sliced
2 tsp finely chopped parsley
1 tsp finely chopped dill
10g capers
grated zest of 1 lemon

METHOD

To make the pastry, rub the flour, butter and salt together using your fingers, until it resembles fine crumbs. Make a well and add the egg, mixing until the mixture forms a dough, adding a little water if needed to bring it together. Shape the dough into a ball, wrap it in cling film and chill in the fridge for at least 30 minutes.

Preheat the oven to 160ºC. Grease a deep 20cm loose-bottomed flan tin (it needs to be at least 2.5cm deep).

Lightly flour a work surface. Roll out the pastry to about 5mm thick and use it to line the tin, leaving a small overhang. Rest in the fridge for another 30 minutes.

Prick the base of the chilled pastry case all over, line it with baking parchment and baking beans. Place in the oven and bake blind for 30 minutes, until light golden, then remove from the oven, lift out the paper and beans and brush the inside of the case with the beaten egg, then return the case to the oven and bake for a further 2 minutes, until golden brown. Remove from the oven and leave to cool while you make the filling.

Turn the oven down to 145ºC.

For the filling, mix the cream, brown crab meat, eggs and egg yolk together until thoroughly combined. Season with 2 dashes of Tabasco and 2 of Worcestershire sauce, then add the cayenne. Pour into the pastry case and bake in the oven for 35–40 minutes or until the filling is set. Chill before slicing and serving.

When ready to serve, gently mix all the topping ingredients together and spoon over the top of the tart. Garnish the top with pea shoots and serve with summer leaves.

Geranium leaf sorbet
with shortbread

MAKES 500G SORBET (TO SERVE 5-6)

225g caster sugar
500ml water
12 sweet-leaved geranium leaves (see below)
juice of 2 limes
1 medium egg white, whipped (optional)

FOR THE SHORTBREAD

300g plain flour, plus extra to dust
200g unsalted butter
100g golden caster sugar
a few drops of cold water

METHOD

To make the sorbet, place the sugar and water in a medium saucepan. Bring to the boil, then add the geranium leaves and the lime juice. Stir, then turn off the heat and leave to cool.

Once completely cool, pass the mixture through a fine sieve. Place in an ice cream machine and churn until smooth. You can add the whipped egg white halfway through churning for a lighter, smoother sorbet if you like. The texture without it is more like a granita.

To make the shortbread, place the flour, butter and sugar in the bowl of a food processor. Whizz briefly, adding a few drops of cold water, until the dough just comes together. Turn out of the bowl and knead very lightly to an even dough. Shape into a thick disc, cover and chill for at least 30 minutes.

Line a baking tray with baking parchment. Dust a clean worktop with a little flour and roll out the dough to 0.5cm thick. Use cutters to cut out biscuits, placing them on the lined tray with plenty of space between them. Lightly knead any leftover dough and roll out to shape more biscuits. Chill for 30 minutes before baking.

Preheat the oven to 160ºC. Once hot, bake the shortbread for 15 minutes or until they are just cooked and have turned a light golden colour. Carefully transfer to a cooling rack.

Remove the sorbet from the freezer about 15 minutes before you'd like to serve it to allow it to soften.

The flavour of the sorbet is a good match for soft summer berries, and melon (depending on where you are in the world). You can use any sweet-leaved geranium for the sorbet – rose geranium varieties work well, but any scented variety lends it a wonderfully fragrant finish.

Cashew 'cheesecake'
with strawberry compote

SERVES 8-8910

1¼ tsp agar agar powder
120ml water
300g cashew nuts
150ml almond milk (or any nut milk of your choice)
60g caster sugar
juice of 1½ lemons
2 tsp vanilla extract
grated zest of 1 lemon
grated nutmeg, to taste
¼ tsp salt
125g coconut oil

FOR THE BASE

70g pumpkin seeds
80g dried dates
50g almonds
20g puffed rice cereal
½ tsp ground cinnamon or mixed spice
1 heaped tsp good-quality cocoa powder
1 tsp vanilla extract
½ tbsp maple syrup
coconut sugar or demerara or soft ligh brown sugar, to taste

FOR THE COMPOTE

250g strawberries, hulled and halved
2 tbsp caster sugar
1 tbsp lemon juice

METHOD

To make the base, preheat the oven to 165ºC fan. Place all the ingredients in a food processor and blitz until the mixture has the consistency of coarse sand; it should come together in your palm.

Spread the mixture over the bottom of a 20cm springform cake tin; it should be about 5-7mm thick. Bake in the oven for 15–20 minutes – you will know it's ready when you notice a slight wobble in the centre but the edges will be firm. Remove and leave to cool.

Put the agar agar and water into a small pot over a medium heat. Bring up to a boil and leave to simmer for 2 minutes to cook it through, while stirring continuously, then remove from the heat and set aside.

Place all the remaining ingredients except the coconut oil in a high-speed blender. Blend on a high speed until silky smooth, then add the coconut oil and blend again. Add the cooked agar agar to the blender and blend well again. Pour the mixture into the cake tin and place in the freezer to set for 2 hours, then refrigerate until ready to serve.

To make the strawberry compote, put the strawberries, sugar and lemon juice into a small pan with 1–2 tablespoons of water, cover and bring to the boil, stirring occasionally until the strawberries soften, then take off the heat and leave to cool. Serve alongside the cheesecake, or dolloped on top of each slice.

Don't be put off by the lack of dairy – the rich, sweet cashews ensure that the texture of this dessert is very similar to that of a standard dairy cheesecake .

HOW SUSTAINABLE ARE OUR COFFEE CHOICES?

WORDS Lizzie Rivera
PHOTOGRAPHY Jocelyn Morales

I love coffee. I account for at least three of the 55 million cups we drink daily in the UK. Each morning, a cup of coffee signals the start of the day. The ceremony of making coffee offers welcome pauses for reflection (and procrastination) during long working hours. I drink coffee late into the afternoon, and after dinner. There's a cafetière sitting beside me as I write this, as darkness falls quietening the world around me, leaving just me, my computer and my coffee.

Which brings us to the now unavoidable question, how sustainable is my habit?

Let's start with the figures. When it comes to black coffee's carbon footprint, it's about four times less sustainable than a cup of tea, according to carbon expert Mike Berners-Lee's book *How Bad are Bananas?* [1]. Make that an oat milk latte, and you're tripling its impact. A dairy milk latte has almost double the carbon footprint again.

I take some solace in the fact that I'm a purist, so I drink my coffee black and without sugar. But, unfortunately, *How Bad are Bananas?* is akin to opening Pandora's box, and suddenly I have the carbon numbers for all our life decisions at my fingertips. The book reveals that the carbon footprint of our coffee really is quite insignificant if we're going to continue to book flights (a return short-haul flight such as from London to Glasgow is 368kg CO_2e (carbon footprints are expressed as 'CO_2e' – carbon dioxyde equivalent – as the figure takes into account the impact of all greenhouse gas emissions – carbon dioxide, methane and nitrous oxide), buy new cars (11 tonnes CO_2e is generated in the production of a Renault Zoe electric

COFFEE CARBON FOOTPRINT IN NUMBERS

Black coffee
(Tea is just 22g)
87G
CO_2e

•

Oat milk latte
288G
CO_2e

•

Soya milk latte
308G
CO_2e

•

Cow's milk latte
552G
CO_2e

A disposable cup would add another 110g CO_2e to each of these figures.

car, increasing to 25 tonnes CO_2e for a Range Rover Sport HSE), or regularly shop for new clothes (up to 19kg CO_2e is produced in the manufacture of a new pair of men's jeans and this figure doesn't take into account the subsequent carbon emissions across its lifecycle: washing, drying etc.). All of this led me to rethink the question: does our coffee choice really matter?

The answer is yes. Firstly, Berners-Lee suggests that everyone in Europe should currently be aiming for a 5-tonne lifestyle, which means that we should each budget for only 5-tonnes of carbon expenditure a year. In a world where one return long-haul flight can use up 90 per cent of your carbon budget, every one of the remaining 500kg of CO_2e is precious.

Plus, while the carbon footprint of a single cup of coffee may feel environmentally insignificant (see the table left) it's the second most popular drink in the world after water so its total impact is not.

Most importantly, it matters to the 25 million coffee farmers worldwide. And yet too often the human story is removed from the sustainability narrative in our race to 'carbon neutral' or 'net zero'. Almost 95 per cent of coffee farms are smaller than five hectares, and 84 per cent of all coffee farms are smaller than two hectares. At this size, farmers struggle to reach an income level above the poverty line [2].

The fact that I even ask, 'Does my coffee choice really matter?' shows how far removed we are from where our coffee really comes from; and blind to the very real impact our choices have on farmers' lives across the globe.

Without a doubt, the biggest issue with coffee globally is the impact of the climate crisis on coffee farms, which is increasing the prevalence of pests and diseases, such as the fungus known as coffee rust that thrives in higher temperatures.

But as Bernard Njoroge, Fairtrade's senior programme officer for Kenya and proud coffee farmer, explains, the second biggest issue for Kenyan coffee farmers is the disconnect with the consumer. As customers, we simply don't think about how the beans get to the UK and this disengagement is problematic because the majority of farmers are exploited. They're locked in supply chains where they are paid very little and have very little agency to change the system.

Currently farmers only receive 0.4 per cent of the price we pay for a cup of coffee in a coffee shop [3], which means the average non-Fairtrade farmer earns as little as £1.37 per day [3], resulting in a daily struggle to pay school fees and put food on the table for the family. 'It would be lovely for me to sit with you and share a cup of coffee from my farm,' Njoroge tells me. If we understood where our coffee came from better, then perhaps the power and economic dynamics would shift. Coffee-drinkers would better appreciate its value if we recognised the hard work and skill that goes into producing coffee, from cherry bush to cup – and the farmers wouldn't be invisible to the consumer, so would have more power to negotiate for a fairer deal.

One reason farmers can't command higher prices is that they are at the far end of a long supply chain. The other is that coffee is a commodity crop widely traded on the New York Stock Exchange, as such the price of coffee is not only determined by supply and demand. Speculation leads to volatility in prices and the price changes every three minutes, reports Fairtrade's senior supply chain manager for coffee Emma Mullins. 'How can farmers plan for the future?' she asks.

Over the last year, coffee prices have hit a 10-year high, rising 78% within a year to just over $2.39/lb (£1.73/lb) [4]; for the decade prior, they were fluctuating at around $1/lb (75p/lb). [4] 'The price of coffee is going up, but the cost of producing coffee is also rising all the time because of the climate crisis and, now, Covid. Pesticide costs, labour costs and logistical costs have all increased, so higher prices do not necessarily translate into a higher income for farmers,' insists Mullins. In a vicious cycle, coffee farmers who don't earn enough to invest in future-proofing their crops from the worst of climate change are bearing the brunt of the crisis.

So, how do you make the right choice when it comes to buying coffee?

'Love what you buy and then make sure that what you're consuming is enhancing livelihoods,' says Violeta Stevens, MD of Union coffee, founded 20-years ago to source speciality coffee responsibly. 'If you have a great quality product that you really enjoy, and the ethics are there, that's a winning combination for everybody involved.' It can be difficult to tell the responsible coffee brands apart from the ones that are doing little more than greenwashing but a few crucial questions a brand's sustainability pages should have clear answers to include: how much do they pay their farmers? Are they building long-term relationships with them? Do farmers have a say in how the business is run as, for example, they do at Cafédirect, a coffee brand that works in partnership, and shares profits, with their farmers.

Third-party certification is another helpful differentiator. There are many certification labels out there – some better than others – but broadly speaking, organic coffee is grown sustainably and Fairtrade guarantees a fairer price for the farmer by setting a minimum price they are paid for their coffee regardless of its market price. Farmers also receive a Fairtrade Premium, 25 per cent of which must be used to enhance productivity, quality or enhance sustainable agricultural practices. Njoroge couldn't be clearer: 'When you're buying Fairtrade you're increasing the value of life to the farmer. They will have more income. Their health will be better. He or she will be able to send their children to school. They will be able to farm more sustainably, increasing their productivity and ensuring they will be in business for years to come.'

Fairtrade also provides technical support and helps farmers to build better relationships with buyers. Mullins explains: 'It's about businesses entering into a relationship with producers rather than extracting from them – treating them with the credibility and respect they deserve.'

In the UK, there are also coffee brands that have social missions. Redemption Roasters trains prisoners with the aim of reducing reoffending and Change Please is a social enterprise that invests 100% of its profits into giving people experiencing homelessness a living wage job, housing and training.

So, does our coffee choice really matter? Yes, it does. When you next put kettle on to boil (with only enough water for the cup you need), or you're waiting for your small oat milk latte (because you're conscious of your carbon footprint), maybe you can think about the farmer who planted the cherry trees and harvested their beans, and consider the impact our decisions have on the people who bring us the morning pick-me-up we value so much.

Lizzie Rivera is a sustainability journalist and founder of sustainable website, Live Frankly www.livefrankly.co.uk

[1] *How Bad are Bananas?*, Mike Berners-Lee (London, Profile Books)

[2] Coffee Barometer 2020 report: https://coffeebarometer.org/

[3] https://www.fairtrade.org.uk/wp-content/uploads/2021/02/A-Climate-Of-Crisis_Fairtrade-Foundation_Feb-2020_HR.pdf

[4] https://www.macrotrends.net/2535/coffee-prices-historical-chart-data

WABI

WORDS Axel Vervoordt and Tatsuro Miki
PHOTOGRAPHY Laziz Hamani

Axel Vervoordt is one of the world's most acclaimed collectors of art and antiques. His taste for spectacular art is counterbalanced by his quest for simplicity, a search that is perhaps best illustrated and defined by his respect for the Japanese culture of Wabi – a concept that celebrates the beauty in authenticity, simplicity and imperfection. In this extract from his atmospheric book *Wabi Inspirations*, Vervoordt and a long-standing collaborator, architect Tatsuro Miki outline the values behind their interpretation of the wabi philosophy and share examples of the Vervoordt interiors that have been inspired by its principles.

Axel Vervoordt
Ever since I was a boy, I have been enthralled by the beauty found in nature's artistry. My room was always filled with little treasures I had lovingly collected – objets trouvés from the forest, fields or seashore.

To this day I still prize pebbles, rocks or old pieces of wood almost as much as I value art. Alongside this love of nature, I have always experienced a deep emotion when I see nobility in poor, humble objects like a shepherd's table carved by time and man, or a piece of pottery transformed by the process of firing. I am particularly intrigued by the similarities found in the work of shepherds or monks from faraway places like the mountains of China, the high Pyrenees, or the Andes in South America; craftsmen who gained their sense of proportion by looking at the stars.

This affection for unpretentious things is heightened by my love for the imperfections found in these objects, along with an attachment to the emotive qualities evident in an unfinished painting or an incomplete sculpture.

In my late twenties, I began to take an intense interest in Chinese Taoism, Japanese Zen Buddhist teachings and Korean philosophy and art. It was through Zen's profound spiritual insights that I first encountered the concept of wabi-sabi, which I read about in Leonard Koren's book on the subject, *Wabi-Sabi: for Artists, Designers, Poets & Philosophers*, as well as Jun'ichirō Tanizaki's *In Praise of Shadows*.

I have had the good fortune to meet and discuss the tenets of Eastern philosophy with many learned scholars, artists and designers. After I started collaborating on a number of projects with the Japanese architect Tatsuro Miki – or Taro as he is know – it was immediately apparent that the two of us shared the same philosophy. Through his talent and insight, Taro has helped us to refine our approach to our work and architecture, an approach that we have called Wabi.

This is a name that we have borrowed from the Japanese term for something that is in its simplest and most natural state: the beauty found in objects that are humble and unassuming.

Through our ongoing dialogue, I have developed a much more perceptive understanding of Japanese concepts and design principles as well as the profound philosophy of Wabi itself.

I have learned that the original spirit of Wabi evolved out of the fundamental values prized by Zen monks who sought solace and contentment in simplicity, purity, restraint and humility. All presided over by the prevailing influence of the impermanence of life.

My own personal concept of Wabi has been fashioned by the Japanese ability to seek inspiration and harmony from nature. Wabi in itself is timeless – without a past, present or future. And through its wisdom it creates a heightened consciousness of space, emptiness and silence. A key aspect of Wabi is the effect a well-designed space has on the psychological wellbeing of the occupant.

Modern living spaces are so often defined by fashion and commercial marketing strategies. But Wabi is not a style, a fashion or a design trend. Neither is it an idea that is likely to be imitated or replicated on a large scale. It is tranquil, calm and reassuring – completely centred. For this stillness is based on ancient wisdom.

Tatsuro Miki: Growing from the roots
The first steps on the path to a way of Wabi. Axel's initial restoration project in the Vlaeykensgang: a series of narrow alleyways and Renaissance houses that wind through Antwerp's historic old quarter. These concealed, almost secret, passageways had fallen into serious disrepair until discovered and bought by Axel in 1968, when he was just 21. With all his passion and zeal he set about conserving the heart and soul of these long-forgotten houses. The main bedroom of his son Boris's house, in particular, has an understated nobility through its Wabi spirit. Every aspect appears so natural, so down to earth. The walls are lined with old recycled wood. Looking up from the bed there is a breathtaking view of Antwerp Cathedral's Gothic spire. Towering in the sky it appears like an omnipresent medieval icon positioned in striking contrast to the calm, welcoming ambience of this Wabi space.

Living art

The medieval castle of 's-Gravenwezel exudes an indescribable beauty. Contemporary yet classical, there is the feeling that these inspirational Wabi rooms have always been part of the castle's centuries-old legacy. With their austere elegance, these spaces draw their inspiration not only from traditional Japanese design but from many other worlds too. For here in this castle different cultures freely collide.

Yet these are calm, tranquil rooms that seem to have evolved in a natural, unforced way: understated but salient spaces designed for quiet contemplation and reflection. Although Axel has ensured that old-fashioned comfort has not been overlooked.

There is a lightness and joy in Wabi that not only incites the mind but gladdens the heart. Unassuming and free from embellishments, ostentation or overworked decoration, these rooms give an uplifting sense of spiritual freedom. This conscious restraint means the understated becomes even more special. Even the imperfections found in everyday objects or furniture take on a special significance.

It follows that traditional decorating methods are used everywhere: earthen walls, timber from the estate, and natural fabrics provide tactile textures with warmth and worthiness – noble organic materials which are fundamental to the Wabi aesthetic.

Extract taken from *Wabi Inspirations*
by Axel Vervoordt (Paris: Flammarion, 2010)

PASTURES NEW

Environmental innovation and regeneration is bringing positive change to the Cotswolds, the much-loved corner of quintessential English countryside

WORDS Harriet O'Brien

Gently rounded hills fold into leafy valleys where honey-stone houses cluster around ancient village churches and handsome old inns exude geniality. The Cotswolds is consummately arcadian England. Covering some 2,000 square kilometres, this rural region in the heart of Britain is about the size of Tenerife in the Canary Islands – swap black sand for green fields and miles of drystone walls. Designated an Area of Outstanding Natural Beauty (AONB) in 1966 in recognition of its rich and diverse landscape, today the Cotswolds remains the largest of 46 similarly protected AONBs in England, Wales and Northern Ireland, its pastoral beauty carefully preserved. Especially in the current, Covid-recovery climate there's a palpable mood of restoration and reawakening here. A number of conservation projects and measures to revitalise the environment are boosting the appeal of the region even more – and adding a sense of sustainability and innovation too.

Prime among them is the Glorious Cotswold Grasslands, a scheme to restore wildflower meadows across the region. Frothy, marvellously named lady's bedstraw, vigorous yellow rattle and bird's-foot trefoil – whose flowers look like tiny yellow slippers – are among the tapestry of species once again thriving on the Cotswolds' limestone soil. Beyond the visual charm is serious purpose. 'We're restoring an ecosystem,' says Harvey Sherwood, who heads the project. He explains that this not just a scheme about flora, but fauna too – in the long term. It requires a great deal of work – surveying soil, sowing and more – to re-establish the stretches of wildflowers that once used to grow here, and then, says Sherwood, much patience is needed before invertebrates, from butterflies to bees, start to return, followed by birds, bats and other animals.

Back in the 1930s about 40 per cent of the Cotswolds was wildflower grassland. Over ensuing decades much of this was destroyed as a result of the use of agrochemicals and other changing practices of land management. Devised by the Cotswolds AONB, the grasslands project was launched in 2019 with the aim of recreating 100 hectares of wildflower-rich landscape. It was heralded as one of the most ambitious such endeavours the country had seen.

What a triumph, then, that by the start of 2022 more than double the original target had been reached, with 210 hectares of wildflower grassland restored – on farms, on verges, on estates (including the National Trust's Dyrham Park and Sherborne Park Estate). Meantime the project has been extended indefinitely – so there's far more to come. And, says Sherwood, the extension has given him time and scope to develop a much-needed system for aftercare. His plans to offer guided walks around some of

A cottage at The Wild Rabbit, Kingham

The Scenic Supper, near Moreton-in-Marsh

the sites were delayed because of the pandemic but they will take shape in due course, with details to be posted on the Cotswolds AONB website.

The Glorious Cotswold Grasslands project very much reflects the growing spirit of regeneration in the region – and the inspiring mood of eco-friendliness, to be found here, too. Enthusiasm for sustainability dates back at least a couple of decades, perhaps most notably with the launch of Daylesford Organic's farm shop in 2002, and this has been boosted during the pandemic; lockdown, in particular, engendered a renewed appreciation of what's right on the doorstep.

There's an ingenious celebration of (very) local produce and fabulous Cotswold views at a brilliantly conceived new enterprise, The Scenic Supper. Owners Toby Baggott and Sam Lawson-King lost jobs in the hospitality industry at the start of the pandemic but not daunted, dreamt up this restaurant venture in response to subsequent social distancing restrictions. Diners eat in small greenhouses, taking in a compelling panorama while being served a feast of modern British fare from a kitchen housed in a recycled shipping container. Based on a hillside at Todenham Manor Farm, The Scenic Supper overlooks an intensely beautiful patchwork of cow- and sheep-grazed pastures near Moreton-in-Marsh.

With ebullience and delight Baggot explains that the restaurant was set up at the farm in part to work with this major supplier – and that reflects an intrinsic ethos of mutual support. 'Within our restaurant environment we've created an incredibly strong sense of community,' he says, adding that he and Lawson-King have known each other since their Cotswold school days and work with an extended yet close-knit local team. The greenhouses, for instance, are designed by Baggott and made by a carpenter friend. This year there are nine of them, including two seating up to eight. They've also expanded the business to include weddings and events – all supported by local suppliers, entertainers and artisan producers.

About 20 minutes' drive south is Kingham, the quintessential Cotswold village set around a large traditional green. It is home to The Wild Rabbit inn, part of the Daylesford enterprise. In addition to bedrooms in the main building, the boutique country pub offers self-catering accommodation in nine village cottages, four of which were acquired and restored in 2020 (two more are under refurbishment at the time of writing). Beams and stone walls have been stripped back and left exposed to highlight the original architecture; bespoke contemporary furniture, crafted locally, contrasts with antique pieces; and among other eco-sensitive measures, roofs are insulated using sheep's wool from the Daylesford estate. Perhaps most appealing of all are details that reuse and recycle elements from the farm – hooks of hazel wood crafted from fallen trees, and handles made from antlers found on Daylesford's sister estate in Staffordshire.

The Wild Rabbit

A deep regard for the area is very much at the heart of the newly-rescued The Lamb Inn at Shipton-under-Wychwood near Chipping Norton; conservation, too. The sixteenth-century pub was in urent need of repair when Peter Creed and Tom Noest took it on in March 2021. In particular, says Creed, the roof had partly rotted. Restoration was a streamlined effort that took place over just a few months – not only reroofing but rewiring as well as redevising the interior (from curtains made by Creed's mother to headboards crafted locally for the 10 bedrooms).

Noest and Creed made a name for themselves when they restored The Bell Inn at Langford, north of Faringdon, in 2017. They have infused The Lamb Inn with their trademark sense of cosy foodieness, with warm shades of red, green and blue, artwork by local friends and a menu featuring venison from Cornbury Park estate up the road. There's a down-to-earth vibe, too, especially at the old-school bar area. Creed and Noest very much welcome those popping in for a pint. 'We aim to breathe new life into the heart of the community,' says Creed.

Restoring once-loved venues has also become a passion for Fred Hicks and Harry (or Baz) Henriques. The duo grew up in the Cotswolds, gained a reputation for innovation and creativity producing street food in London and in effect have evolved into their own brand, Baz & Fred. In 2019 they returned to the Cotswolds and revamped the ailing Hare and Hounds inn on the Fosse Way near Cirencester, renaming it The Stump (its local nickname) and redevising it as a pizza pub – with flamboyant style. Happy crowds descended.

In lockdown Baz & Fred acquired The New Inn, a neglected 500-year-old ivy-clad tavern tucked away at nearby Coln St Aldwyns. This the duo has resurrected as a high-end burger and small plates pub with 15 luxury bedrooms and a warm vibe; hardly the most predictable combination but it's proved a winning

The Lamb Inn, Shipton-under-Wychwood

one. 'We stripped away years of horrible paint,' says Fred, 'and restored the dynamic of the pub by reinstating a proper bar for locals.' Indeed there's an emphasis on going local – from suppliers (whether meat and veg or drinks such as Hook Norton ales), to artworks and furnishings of pews and other finds from nearby antique shops.

In 2021 Baz & Fred expanded to include a wedding venue, Old Gore Barn, just off the Fosse Way. And there's more from the unstoppable partners: in picturesque Bibury they have transformed an unloved bric-a-brac shop into an appealing little café. The Twig serves coffee from Ue roastery in the Cotswolds and serves a cornucopia of cakes and pastries made nearby. Visiting in winter, just after it opened, there was already a buzz here and clearly much appreciation and support from local customers. Such are the joys of regeneration.

The New Inn, Coln St Aldwyns

cotswoldsaonb.org.uk, thewildrabbit.co.uk, thescenicsupper.co.uk, thelambshipton.com, bazfred.com

ON THE UP

WORDS Anna Turns
PHOTOGRAPHY Edwin Tan

From mushrooms grown in disused underground car parks in Paris to harvests of micro herbs in two old air raid shelters beneath London's Clapham South tube station, hi-tech, climate-controlled indoor farms are popping up in unlikely places. Are they indicative of what sustainable food production will look like in the future, or does the environmental footprint negate any potential benefits of growing this way?

Stacked high with industrial-scale shelving full of green plants, these futuristic indoor farms – known as vertical farms – are more like ultra-efficient labs than a farmer's open fields. In the absence of natural sunlight, plants such as salad leaves, leafy greens and herbs are grown without soil, using hydroponic or mineral nutrient solutions, in mediums made of coconut coir, porous clay pellets or a rock-based mineral fibre known as rockwool, which supports the root system. The plants are fed nutrients via water and the growing season is extended with carefully-selected LED light recipes. Everything is closely monitored and controlled, from the temperature to the combination of micronutrients fed to each crop.

Also known as 'controlled environment agriculture', vertical farms claim to be sustainable in many ways. Inside, there's no risk of unwanted pests so no pesticides are required, crops are grown 365 days of the year, and the controlled indoor systems are 'closed loop', which means that resources don't escape into the wider environment. Water, for example, is used to irrigate the plants, then captured and re-used so there's no effluent polluting the surrounding land or waterways, as there would be to some extent with any conventional farming model. Water consumption is minimal because rainwater is captured then reused. Yields aren't affected by extreme weather events and so could provide a more resilient way to farm in the face of the climate crisis. Plus these facilities use much less space to produce a harvest, so rural land could potentially be freed up.

But is this novel way of farming really scalable? James Lloyd-Jones of Jones Food Company, Europe's largest vertical farm, thinks so. He looks beyond urban space to make his business financially viable. 'I wouldn't put our farms in cities because the land is too expensive,' says Lloyd-Jones who opened his first vertical farming facility in Scunthorpe, Lincolnshire in November 2018. At the time, it was the world's largest, covering the same area as 26 tennis courts with 17 layers of herbs growing in vertical stacks. Another facility at Lydney, Gloucestershire, three times the size, will become the world's biggest vertical farm when it opens later this year.

'To be part of the supply chain, vertical farms need to be plant factories: they need to just do one thing really well; just like a farmer's field. So, we're optimising production constantly and Scunthorpe produces 180 tonnes of basil per annum. That's between 30–50 per cent of the UK's cut basil that goes into 3,000 supermarkets every single week,' says Lloyd-Jones. Vertical farming is already a big part of the food supply chain because all non-organic salad leaves, and many herbs grown in the UK are produced at indoor facilities like this one. 'You've probably been eating our products for the past four years without realising it,' he says. However, Lloyd-Jones's mission is not to produce enough food solely through vertical farms to feed the entire world. He explains that the key issue with sustainability of the global food systems is not one of productivity – we already grow enough food but one third of it gets wasted, so ultimately, it's a distribution problem. Lloyd-Jones is convinced that vertical farms, which shorten supply chains, can improve food security and reduce the need for imports. With more vertical farming hubs across the country, he hopes that a more regionalised food system will be less dependent on the convoluted, globalised supply chains pushed to their limits by Brexit or Covid-19. And while most large-scale agriculture is under increasing pressure due to soaring natural gas prices (natural gas is required to make most commercial nitrogen fertiliser), this doesn't worry Lloyd-Jones who only uses 'small amounts' of traditional nitrogen fertilisers.

Critics claim that indoor farming at this scale costs an extortionate amount in energy because the system relies on LED lighting for 365 days of the year as there's no natural sunlight. Lloyd-Jones has installed solar farms, primarily because it makes business sense. 'Modern conventional farms use a lot of power too; it's not just one tractor in a field,' he says. Actually, energy consumption is widely considered to be huge in vertical farms but the specifics are often vague. The recent global CEA (controlled environment agriculture) census report concluded that there's 'more work to be done around transparency' across this sector – more data needs to be captured and published to track progress and prove any sustainability claims.

The facility at Lydney will grow more herbs and salad leaves but Lloyd-Jones says anything is possible: 'You can grow anything, it just depends on what you're going to pay for it. Now, it's about building capacity and we have plans for cut flowers, soft fruits, possibly even vines and hops. I reckon we're 10–15 years off doing wheat at a production price. It's about economies of scale.' As this advanced agri-tech gets cheaper and gradually more mainstream, the possibilities could grow.

But Patrick Holden, founding director of the Sustainable Food Trust argues that although vertical farming is 'a beguiling idea', it isn't real food. 'We've already crossed the rubicon into a hydroponic world and the consequences are playing out in a second generation of people with impaired physical health because of their nutrition. Fundamentally, the soil is the stomach of any plant – think of your own digestion and the incredibly complex symbiotic relationship between all the microbes in your gut,' he explains. 'Without that, we wouldn't be as healthy as we are. That microbiome in our own body is well-understood but meanwhile we seem quite happy to abandon that whole thing when it comes to plant nutrition. That's the weirdest thing.' He compares hydroponics to feeding a patient through a stomach tube: 'Can you keep them alive in hospital with nutrients in solution? Yes, but is it the same as a truly healthy digestive system which involves all these subtle micronutrients which are the result of this miraculous symbiotic digestive process? No, it isn't.'

Lloyd-Jones argues that while there's always a risk of missing out on healthy soil microbes, food could be growing in contaminated soil in a greenhouse or on the land, and that could affect gut health in a negative way: 'The products we grow have high nutritional value, we know because we test them, and many of your peppers, tomatoes and cucumbers have been grown hydroponically in massive greenhouses for 30 years.'

UK and EU legislation rules that plants grown in vertical farms without the use of pesticides cannot be certified organic because they haven't been grown in soil. In the US, however, hydroponically grown crops can be classed as organic. 'The whole point of organic is that it's soil-based,' argues Holden who worries that there's an underlying cultural issue of disconnect too. 'We are what we eat, we are related to the soil, but that connection between food and nature is being severed. There are profound consequences to that, in terms of both physical and mental health. Health isn't just the absence of disease, it's about resilience. To build long-term health, we need to grow real food.'

The UK's leading organic certifier, the Soil Association is calling for the international organic movement to prohibit hydroponics in organic agriculture because by their very nature, vertical farms can't be considered regenerative, don't actively replenish soil health, encourage more wildlife or reduce flood risks. But Sarah Compson, international development manager in the Soil Association's standards team does acknowledge that hydroponics are, 'a welcome departure from conventional pesticide-intensive agriculture' and could have 'a significant place' in a more sustainable food future.

Vertical farming certainly isn't a silver bullet but Jess Davies, professor of sustainability at Lancaster University, sees huge potential for the UK to undergo an urban agricultural revolution and for more unused spaces to be transformed and used as places where food is grown. She talks of 'radical rurbanisation' and wants to redefine that line between rural and urban areas: 'We have developed into this food system that has intensive agriculture in a rural environment close to our natural resources and nature, then very concentrated urban environments devoid of food growing so there's no connection between where we grow and what we eat. We want to bring some of that back into cities and see what benefits that brings with it, beyond just calories, in terms of community and wellbeing.'

Davies believes that low-input, space-saving vertical farms do have a place within a future food system. 'Diversifying our production methods will result in a mix of benefits and it's an interesting complementary mode of growing that could be a way to relieve some of the pressure on our soils,' she explains, if, of course, space freed up isn't used for property development, transport infrastructure or more concrete jungle. She emphasises that it's not homogenous – 'vertical farming can be big, small, centralised or distributed, commercial or socially driven'.

And therein lies the key to a real revolution in agriculture. Diversity of soil microbes creates healthier soils which then support a rich, diverse ecosystem of plants and animals. But vertical farming also has its benefits. A more efficient future food system requires a diverse set of solutions, so while commercially-viable vertical farming remains controversial within the growing sustainable agriculture movement, it's not a black and white argument. Hi-tech vertical farms probably won't ever replace conventional farming completely but by triggering healthy debate, this industry could result in a reimagination of food supply chains that's better for people and the planet.

Velocity

Blue Fire

GROWING TOMATOES SUCCESSFULLY

AT HOME

Learning how to grow tomatoes is a right of passage for any home grower, allotmenteer or smallholder. The hero crop of the summer and a daily ingredient during the warmest part of the season, a basket of home-grown tomatoes is one of the most flavoursome labours of love one can share. I will often suggest to any keen grower that they invest in as large a domestic polytunnel as they can. Growing under the protection of glass or polythene is the best way to create the warm conditions needed to grow and ripen tomatoes, it also means you can protect the crop from 'blight', an often fatal disease that is near impossible to avoid during periods of high humidity in late summer, when you grow tomatoes outside.

WORDS Jez Taylor – PHOTOGRAPHY Martin Morrell

Blue Fire

An unripe Blue Fire

BUSH OR VINE?

Tomato varieties are either 'determinate' with a limited number of branches/shoots on the plant; or 'indeterminate', which means that each shoot will carry on growing unless stopped. The former are referred to as bush types and are generally grown without support, such as in hanging baskets, containers, cold frames or under cloches. The latter are known as vine types because their growth is trained up a string or pole.

In the UK tomatoes are generally grown as a vine inside a polytunnel or glasshouse, or, if you are in the south of the country, in the sunniest, most sheltered part of your garden. They will grow best if planted into soil that has been enriched with plenty of compost. If you can't plant directly into the ground then use as large a container as possible, such as a 35-litre pot filled with compost and ideally some well-rotted farmyard manure to provide slow-release plant food. A larger container can retain more water, so is less prone to drying out.

Many people grow tomatoes in growbags, but unless you can water effectively up to twice a day in hot summer then drying out can be a problem, creating plant stress that can lead to whitefly infestation and fruiting problems such as 'blossom end rot' which is when the end of the fruit (the opposite end to the stalk) doesn't form properly and appears as a scab on the tip of the fruit. Growing in a small volume of compost or soil also limits the amount of plant food available to the plant, so supplementary plant feeding is necessary.

CHOOSING VARIETIES

It takes more energy for plants to produce large fruit than small, so I encourage home growers to grow cherry tomatoes rather than larger varieties. Cherry tomatoes also ripen faster, giving earlier cropping.
The organic hybrid variety Sakura has become the most reliable cherry variety in my repertoire, producing long trusses of fruit from late June. Other cherry stalwarts are Sungold, Black Cherry and Yellow Submarine.

When it comes to larger tomatoes, as a commercial grower I cannot help but appreciate some of the modern organic hybrid varieties that give heavy crops on uniform plants. Varieties such as Pozzano – a large San Marzano/plum type that is great for slicing or cooking down into thick sauces – offer great versatility and productivity at the same time. However, anyone really passionate about tomato-growing needs to delve into the world of heritage varieties. In my experience they produce reliable harvests and work well both in cooking and served raw. Orange Banana, Green and Red Zebra, Purple Russian and Blue Fire are a few of the regulars in our mix at Daylesford.

If blight is a constant issue for you, and you're tired of seeing your crop rotting before it has even started to ripen, or if you are just growing tomatoes outside for the first time, then there are many modern blight-resistant varieties available, such as Primabella, Crimson Crush, Magic Mountain and Losetto.

Goldiana

BASKET/CONTAINER TYPES

If space is limited then a 30cm hanging basket or container with three dwarf tomato plants can be really productive. Tumbler and Tumbling Tom can be grown on in a glasshouse until early June, then put up outside in a sunny/sheltered spot where the green fruit can gradually ripen over a 6–10 week period. If grown in a basket, blight becomes less of an issue because the plants are suspended so air flow is good. The only downside is the need for daily watering and weekly feeding. I always recommend a plant-derived fertiliser made from seaweed or comfrey.

Devotion

EARLY OPPORTUNITIES

If you have a cold frame or an opportunity to place a protective cloche over plants in the ground or in large containers such as a deep trough on a sunny patio, then growing early bush varieties, such as Latah or Red Alert, can give you large volumes of fruit before the blight season kicks in. Humidity is the biggest determinant of blight risk, so generally the further west and north you are (in the UK) the more humid/wet the climate is generally. Plants must be lifted off the floor with straw (like strawberries) to minimise soil splash on to fruit and care must be taken when harvesting not to damage the plant, but all the work of side shooting and training can be avoided, along with the expense of large protective structures, such as greenhouses or polytunnels.

SOURCING TOMATOES

Mail order plant suppliers and garden centres offer a wide range of plant varieties these days, which can take the pain out of growing your own from seed. However, if you do have the time, then germinating tomatoes can be done very easily on a sunny windowsill from late February/early March. It's just important when the seedling is potted on (usually within a month of germination) that it is grown in a frost-free greenhouse, otherwise they can become 'leggy' and weak (plants stretch for the light, so the space between the leaves becomes wider, making the plants look long or 'leggy'). My go-to suppliers are Tamar Organic Seeds and Real Seeds. Be warned that it is quite easy to end up with far more tomato plants than you might have room for, so if you have growing friends then I suggest pooling resources and growing for the group; the grower with the best greenhouse facilities then raises the plants.

Most of the work associated with growing tomatoes is gentle, meditative work, done in the shelter of a greenhouse or polytunnel. As horticulturalists rarely fully retire, I think I will have the opportunity to grow and enjoy some of my finest tomato harvests when I have a little more time to lavish on them later in life.

Jez Taylor has been managing the market garden at Daylesford farm since 2008. He grows hundreds of varieties of fruit and vegetables organically as well as a range of cut flowers.

GROWING VINE TOMATOES

Plant out plants 40cm apart in a row, once the risk of frost has passed.

•

Water regularly, when the soil looks dry. Initially a weekly watering is probably sufficient; it will become more frequent as temperatures increase and the plants get larger.

•

Loosely tie string to the base of the plant, tying the other end to a wire/fixing point 2–2.5m above the base. Alternatively, you can tie the plant to a cane but the former will support its weight better.

•

Each week, wind the plant around the string and remove any side shoots, which occur in the cleft between plant leaves and the plant's main stem, taking care not to damage any flower trusses.

•

As summer progresses, make sure that protected spaces are ventilated to ensure temperatures don't creep too high. Above 30ºC tomatoes can become stressed.

•

As fruit ripens at the base of the plant, remove lower leaves to expose the fruit and improve air flow and deter blight.

•

Water after each time you harvest – this helps limit the amount of fruit that splits.

•

Check for signs of blight (small patches of furry brown mould) on leaves, and remove infected leaves immediately (they're fine on a compost heap). Daily ventilation will also help reduce humidity.

•

At the end of the season, clear all remaining unripe fruit and leave to ripen in a dry, shady space, such as in a seed tray on a shelf in the shed. Or use it to make a green tomato chutney.

GROWING A GARDEN MEADOW

MAKING WILDFLOWER SEED BOMBS WITH CHILDREN

WORDS Leonora Bamford
PHOTOGRAPHY Martin Morrell

I've always been fascinated by seeds. Growing something from a tiny spec in the palm of your hand feels like magic to me and I find so much joy in selecting what to grow, becoming transfixed when little green shoots start to appear.

As a child, during the Easter holidays, my mother would help me and my brothers plant sunflower seeds in little seed trays. We would nurture them daily and when they had grown into seedlings, we would plant them out in the garden then keep a watchful eye on them. I vividly remember staring in amazement as the stems grew and grew, eventually soaring to become taller than us so that we had to secure them to bamboo sticks. We always grew the tall variety, which meant that we could harvest and eat the flowers' seeds. The whole process was exciting and fun and is something I now love doing with my own children.

My mother-in-law's potting shed is one of my children's favourite parts of her garden – it looks like it has fallen out of a Beatrix Potter story – and the children will spend hours with her, choosing what to sow from a wonderful old seed box and listening to her teach them tricks about how best to grow them. They used to tip the whole packet of seeds into one tiny tray, but they've quickly learned to be a bit less generous with the pouring. They've all become rather green-fingered and now look after a whole patch of our garden at home, which has meant that last summer we had more vegetables than we could eat. But it's been such a joy to watch them develop their skills and I love hearing them talk about how they would do things differently next year: 'These lettuces have bolted already – I should have pulled them up last week,' or, 'I planted these carrots far too close together and they're all tangled up around each other.'

A few years ago we were given a wildflower bee bomb and I immediately loved the idea of them. Anyone can throw the balls of seeds out into their garden and as long as they're watered well, flowers will appear. The children and I were amazed at how quickly ours sprouted, so we began making our own. They wanted to create an area of the garden that butterflies would flock to, so we researched the wildflowers that attracted them and tried our luck. Seeds bombs are very easy to make, and lots of fun, though you definitely need to keep your eye on where they end up – my youngest has quite a mighty throw and when my back was turned, he threw one into the vegetable patch that had just been raked for planting. Soon enough little shoots started to appear.

With just a few elements you can make myriad seed bombs and the beauty is that you can choose how to fill them. I stock up on seeds every time I visit a nursery but I've also started taking seeds from my favourite flowers in the garden and keeping them in little brown envelopes – you just have to remember to jot down what's inside.

CRAFT

TO MAKE

Wildflower seed bombs

YOU WILL NEED:

meadow flower seeds
peat-free compost
mixing bowl
scraps of biodegradable fabric
string

In a bowl, mix together a handful of seeds with a couple of handfuls of compost. Slowly mix in a little water with your hands until everything sticks together. You don't want it to be too wet, but moist enough that you can roll the mixture into firm balls. Leave the balls to dry in a sunny spot for as long as possible.

Once dry wrap each ball in a square of fabric and tie with the string. You can gift them as presents, or when you're ready to plant your seed bombs, unwrap them and throw them at bare parts of the garden. Water well and wait to see what grows.

A TABLE FOR SPRING

PHOTOGRAPHY
Martin Morrell

STYLING
Milly Bruce

PREVIOUS PAGES, vases hanging from left to right: stylist's own, Daylesford Stubby Bud vase, stylist's own, Daylesford Acorn vase, stylist's own, Daylesford Ink Bud vase, stylist's own; on the table: Daylesford Drip salad bowls and dinner plates; Daylesford Tiller napkins, lilac; Issy Granger Pom wine glasses, green; Daylesford Tiller tablecloth, white; tumblers and cutlery, stylist's own

ABOVE: Issy Granger Horus glass candlestick; Daylesford Acorn vase

RIGHT: Daylesford Drip salad bowl and dinner plate; Issy Granger Thebes glass candlestick; Daylesford Tiller tablecloth, white

LEFT: Daylesford Drip salad bowl and dinner plate; Issy Granger Pom wine glass, green

ORGANIC FIG LEAF GIN
Fragrant and floral gin distilled with fig leaves and bergamot
BOTTLE DESIGNED BY HUGO GUINNESS

daylesford ORGANIC
WWW.DAYLESFORD.COM

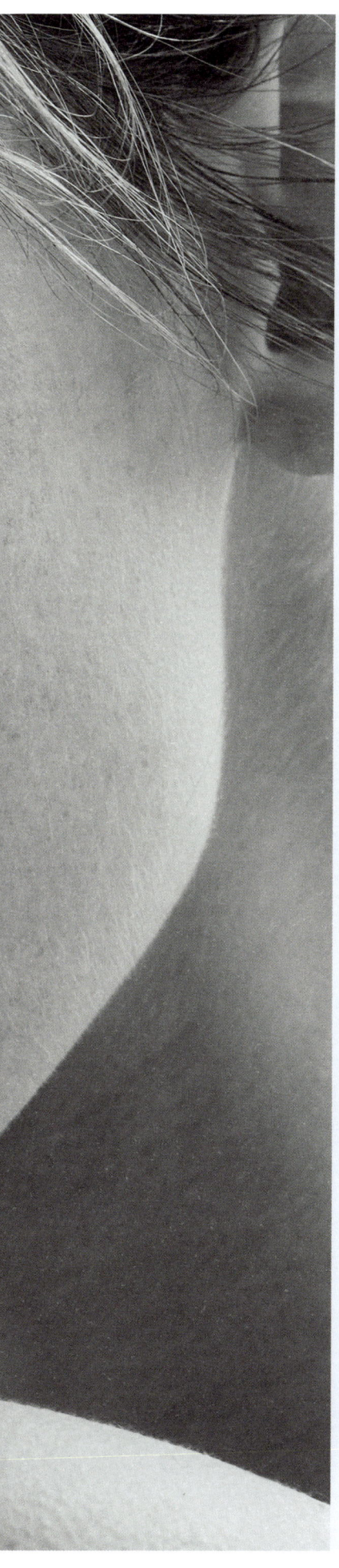

STEM CELL SERUM

PRODUCED USING PLANT-DERIVED BIOTECHNOLOGY, THIS LIGHTWEIGHT SERUM CAPTURES THE REGENERATIVE PROPERTIES OF ALPINE ROSE AND RASPBERRY FOR A RADIANT, SMOOTH COMPLEXION.

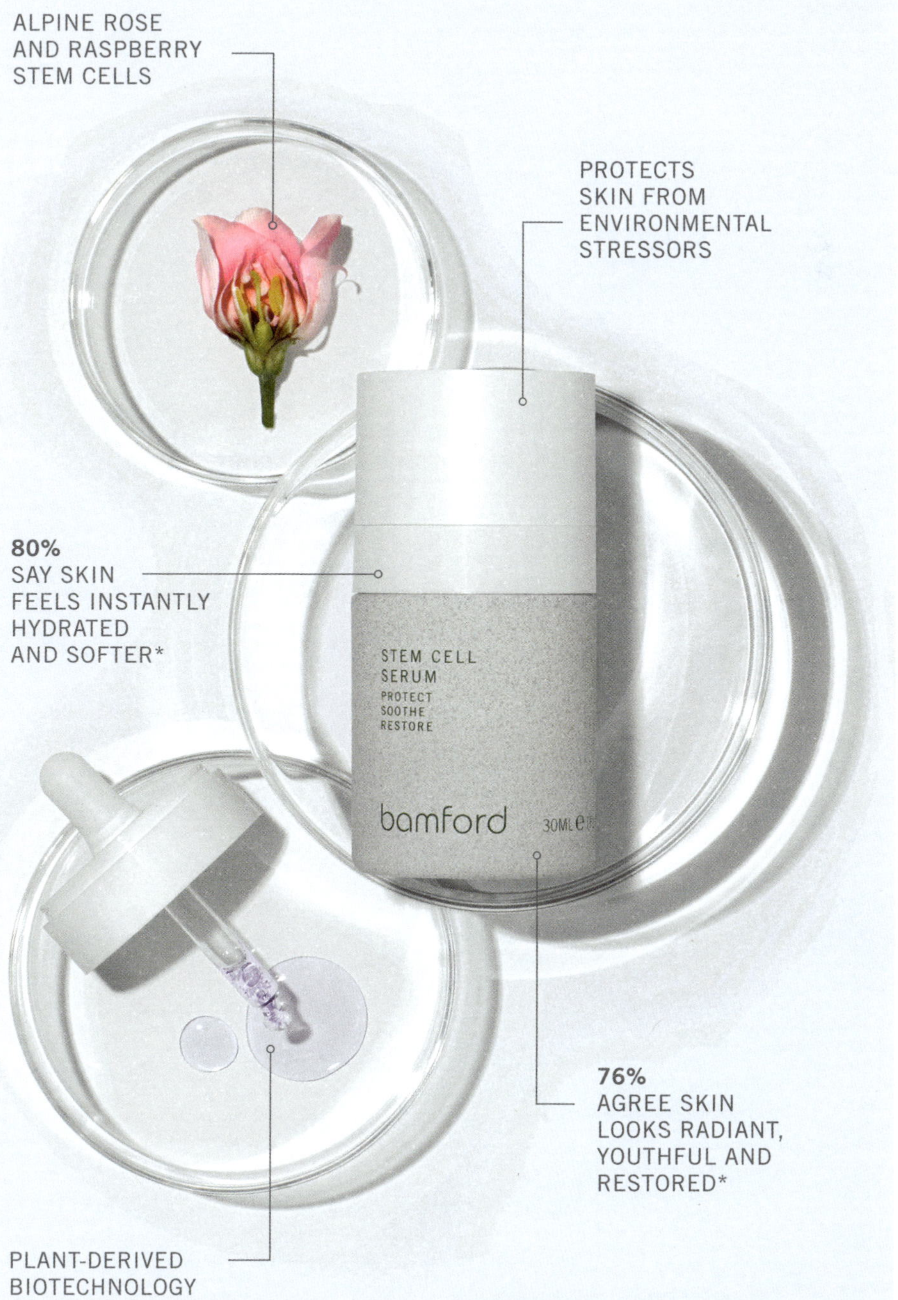

ALPINE ROSE AND RASPBERRY STEM CELLS
PROTECTS SKIN FROM ENVIRONMENTAL STRESSORS
80% SAY SKIN FEELS INSTANTLY HYDRATED AND SOFTER*
STEM CELL SERUM
PROTECT SOOTHE RESTORE
bamford
76% AGREE SKIN LOOKS RADIANT, YOUTHFUL AND RESTORED*
PLANT-DERIVED BIOTECHNOLOGY

* User trial on 50 people over 4 weeks / 28 days

You go nowhere alone

**you are one person
but when you move
an entire community
walks through you**

– Rupi Kaur